What Others are saying abo

"Naomi Lowinsky has given us a remarkable, fearless, and full autobiography. Speaking in poetic, psychologically sensitive, scholarly dialogues with her shape-shifting muse, she has created a new form. Through it she beckons us to attune with her as she explores her own personal and archetypal journeys, sounding the passionate depths of the Self that Everywoman may traverse when she lives authentically. This is a beautiful book to treasure and spread among worthy friends."

—Sylvia Perera, Author of *Descent to the Goddess*
and *Celtic Queen Maeve and Addiction.*

"*The Sister From Below: When the Muse Gets Her Way*, is in part a memoir of the author finding her poetic calling and in part a superb meditation on the creative process itself. Using as her vehicle conversations with various aspects of her own muse(s), Naomi Ruth Lowinsky offers us a superbly detailed investigation of the powerful, mythic forces of the world as they are revealed to the active creative self. Don't miss this enlightening and fascinating book."

—David St. John, Author of *Study for the World's Body:*
New and Selected Poems and *Prism.*

"*The Sister from Below* is a major contribution to active imagination as encounter and dialogue with the gods within. At the same time it is interwoven with stories of travel as pilgrimage, travel as inner journey and travel through time. Naomi's poetry and prose is infused with the suffering and joys of humans everywhere. Insightful and deeply moving, she brings us the food and water of life."

—Joan Chodorow, Author of *Dance Therapy and Depth Psychology,*
editor of *C.G. Jung on Active Imagination.*

"The Sister from Below tells the complex story a woman poet has with her muse—"a nudge, a nag, an intruder, a banshee" demanding her time despite the challenges to her everyday life. Lowinsky brings us the voices of Sappho, Eurydice, the hungry ghost of her grandmother, and others who give her their lives to shape into images. A passionate love letter to those who yearn to be heard. A must read for every woman who longs to write poetry."

—Maureen Murdock, Author of *The Heroine's Journey*
and *Unreliable Truth: On Memoir and Memory.*

"In poetry and prose Naomi Lowinsky has created a biographical self-portrait. Being a sensitive, intelligent woman, born shortly after her German refugee parents escaped the holocaust and moved to the United States, it is little wonder that this child struggled with "being taken over" by emotion-laden forces she calls "her shape-shifting Sister from Below." Slowly these two, Lowinsky and her "Sister," begin to converse, giving birth to poetry.

"The central anchor of the book is located in the chapters related to her paternal grandmother, who died in a concentration camp in Holland—from cancer, not the ovens. Lowinsky makes peace with her grandmother and gains a capacity to bear the unspeakable suffering of her family. Through her recovered vision, she reinterprets mythic and historical reality in provocative versions of the stories of Eurydice, Helen, Ruth, Naomi, and Sappho. The voice of the Sister from Below argues, cajoles, prods, explains, and yes, loves her human counterpart, and becomes the inspiration for Lowinsky's stunning poetry in this highly original book."

—Betty de Shong Meador, Author of *Inanna, Lady of Largest Heart* and *Princess, Priestess, Poet.*

THE SISTER FROM BELOW

THE SISTER FROM BELOW
WHEN THE MUSE GETS HER WAY

NAOMI RUTH LOWINSKY, PH.D.

Fisher King Press
www.fisherkingpress.com
info@fisherkingpress.com
+1-831-238-7799

The Sister from Below: When the Muse Gets Her Way

Copyright © 2009 Naomi Ruth Lowinsky

ISBN 978-0-9810344-2-3

First Edition

Published simultaneously in Canada and the United States of America. For information on obtaining permission for use of material from this work, please submit a written request to: permissions@fisherkingpress.com

Many thanks to all sources that have directly or indirectly provided permission to quote their works, including:

"Eurydice" By H.D. (Hilda Doolitte), from COLLECTED POEMS, 1912-1944, COPYRIGHT © 1982 by The Estate of Hilda Doolittle. Reprinted by permission of New Directions Publishing Corp.

"Black Flakes", "Deathfugue", "Tenebrae", "Psalm", "Radix Matrix", "Zurich, at the Stork", from SELECTED POEMS AND PROSE OF PAUL CELAN by Paul Celan, translated by John Felstiner. Copyright © 2001 by John Felstiner. Used by permission of W.W. Norton & Company, Inc.

"Orpheus, Eurydice, Hermes," translated by Stephen Mitchell, copyright © 1982 by Stephen Mitchell, from THE SELECTED POETRY OF RAINER MARIA RILKE, translated by Stephen Mitchell. Used by permission of Random House, Inc.

Chiron Publications for permission to quote from *Uncursing the Dark* by Betty de Shong Meador (1992).

The cover image, "Phases of the Moon" is an oil painting copyright © by Bianca Daalder-van Iersel.

CONTENTS

The cover image "Phases of the Moon" is an oil painting by Bianca Daalder-van Iersel, an artist and Jungian analyst practicing in Los Angeles, California. Learn more about the artist and her work at www.bdaalder.com.

ACKNOWLEDGMENTS

It is said that it takes a village to raise a child. I can tell you that it has taken a far flung community to bring "The Sister" from manuscript into print. I have been blessed by overlapping circles of Jungians, poets, family and friends who have given good counsel, read drafts, brainstormed, and kept the faith.

My husband, Dan Safran, has been a devoted friend to me and "The Sister"— helpful listener, amazing trip planner, and careful copy editor. My daughter, Shanti Dorfman, saved the day when my notebook from our Indian travels was stolen. I thank her for letting me quote from her beautiful journal. My children, step children, in-laws and grandchildren are always a source of nurture and joy.

Venezuelan poet Alicia Torres made her magical appearance just when I needed an editor. She saw "The Sister's" form before I did.

Robin Robertson has always believed in my writing, and always believed that "The Sister" would find her way into print. His faith has been a gift.

Diane di Prima helped me find my way back to my roots in poetry— another gift.

Leah Shelleda has been a deep friend and companion in poetry. She has seen many versions of most everything I've written. I am also grateful to my friends, the poets Lucy Day, Jane Downs, Patricia Damery, Marilyn Steele, the Deep River circle and the Cloud View Poets—you've provided much advice and encouragement. Thanks also to Cathy Valdez, Carolyn Cowan, Jan Robinson, for listening and caring. I'm forever grateful to Bill Fulton, who feathered my writing nest.

My deep gratitude to Gilda Frantz, Margi Johnson, Margaret Ryan and everyone on the board of Psychological Perspectives. You have given my writing a home. Most of "The Sister" first appeared in the pages of Psychological Perspectives. John Beebe gave my writing its start in the Jungian world. And the late Joseph Henderson helped me believe in my voice.

I am also grateful to my friends and colleagues at the North South meetings of Jungian Analysts, as well as my Jungian friends in Bulgaria, South Africa, Santa Fe, San Diego, Los Angeles, Portland and Seattle, who have been so responsive to earlier versions of this material.

Very special thanks to my friend, Israeli Jungian analyst Erel Shalit, who guided me to Fisher King Press. Thanks to Joseph Pagano, for his enthusiasm and thanks to Patty Cabanas for her scrupulous copy editing. And deep appreciation to my publisher, Mel Mathews for his sensitivity and care for me and "The Sister." Neither one of us thought we'd find a publisher who got us!

Many thanks to Jungian analyst and painter Bianca Daalder, for permission to use her image on the cover.

Eternal gratitude to Gareth Hill and Betty de Shong Meador, midwives to this blossoming.

I am grateful to the editors of *Psychological Perspectives*, *The San Francisco Jung Institute Library Journal*, and the anthology *Terror, Violence and the Impulse to Destroy*, who published some of the chapters of this book in earlier versions.

Chapter 1: The Argument. Parts were first published in *The San Francisco Jung Institute Library Journal*, in the essay "Song of Herself," Vol. 14 no. 1, 1995. Parts were first published in *Psychological Perspectives*, in the essay "The Poetry of Soul," Issue 33, Fall 1995.

Chapter 2: When the Sister Gets Her Way. Parts were first published in *Psychological Perspectives*, in the essay "The Poetry of Soul," Issue 33, Fall 1995.

Chapter 4: How Eurydice Tells It. First published in *Psychological Perspectives*, Issue 38, 1998-1999.

Chapter 5: A Grandmother Speaks from the Other Side. First published as "Wrestling with God: From the Book of Job to the Poets of the Shoah" in *Terror, Violence and the Impulse to Destroy*, ed. John Beebe, Daimon (2002).

Chapter 6: Old Mother India. First published as "The Fire of India" in *Psychological Perspectives*, Issue 41, 2000.

Chapter 8: Helena is a Root Vegetable. First published as "What the Centaur Said" in *Psychological Perspectives*, Issue 45, 2002.

Chapter 9: The Book of Ruth: Naomi's Version. First published as "Thy Gods and Mine," *Psychological Perspectives*, Issue 34, 1996.

Chapter 10: Beloved of the Beloved. First published in *Psychological Perspectives*, Vol. 48, Issue 2, 2005.

On the Muse

The test of a poet's vision....is the accuracy of his portrayal of the White Goddess. The reason why the hairs stand on end, the eyes water, when one writes or reads a true poem is that a true poem is necessarily an invocation of the White Goddess, or Muse, the Mother of All Living . . .

—Robert Graves[1]

Who is this She?

She inserts herself into everything I do. Everyday She insists on time from me, time spent listening to her. Even when I'm busy, on my way to work or preoccupied with the news, She says: "Give me just ten minutes. That's all I ask. Sit in a chair. Take a deep breath. Take pen in your hand and write down what I say!" And you know, I always feel better after I do: more grounded, more real to myself, creative and alive.

Who is this She? She is not about the ordinary business of life: work, shopping, making dinner. She speaks from other realms. If you let Her, She will whisper in your ear, lead your thoughts astray, fill you with strange yearnings, get you hot and bothered, send you off on some wild goose chase of a daydream, eat up hours of your time. For She is a siren, a seductress, a shape-shifter. Why should you listen to such a trouble-maker? Because She is essential to the creative process; She holds the keys to your imagination and your deeper life.

The image of the muse who visits the poet and inspires the creative process is as old as poetry. She has been invoked since the first poet we know, the Sumerian priestess Enheduanna, invoked her fierce goddess, Inanna, four thousand years ago. Homer knew Her and called on her for help. The Greeks knew nine Muses, daughters of Zeus and Mnemosyne, goddess of memory. Their names were Calliope, muse of eloquence and epic poetry, Clio, muse of history and writing, Euterpe, muse of music, Terpsichore, muse of dance, Erato, muse of love poetry, Melpomene, muse of tragedy, Thalia, muse of

---

1 Robert Graves, *The White Goddess*, p. 24.

comedy, Polyhymnia, muse of oratory, sacred hymns, and poetry, and Urania, muse of astronomy and science.[2]

The 6th century BCE Greek poet Alcman, invoked Calliope and declared: "the Muse has raised her voice, the clear voiced Siren." He knew Her to be a dangerous enchantress but essential to his creative process.[3] The great lyric poet Sappho knew Her too, summoning the "Muses/ with lovely hair"[4] to help her transform the torments of love into eloquent song.

Does the muse still visit poets and artists? Or did She disappear when people lost their faith in spirit and myth? Poets do not commonly invoke Her these days, so what manner of being is She who visits me? Do I mean the soul? Do I mean Atman as in Hinduism or the Self as in Jungian psychology? Do I mean inspiration? Or, with Robert Graves, do I mean the Goddess?

When a troubadour praised his Lady, was he invoking the muse? When the alchemists engaged in "meditatio," which they described as an "Internal Talk....with another who is invisible, as in the invocation of the Deity, or.... with one's good angel,"[5] were they being visited by the muse? When C.G. Jung engaged in active imagination with an inner figure he called Philamon, who explained to him the objective reality of the psyche, was he being visited by the muse?[6] When Jacob, his head upon a stone pillow, found himself in the grip of an angel, who wrestled with him all night long, wounded him, and gave him his name, Israel, was he in the presence of the muse? Is an angel a muse? Is the beloved a muse? Is a god a muse? Or is the muse an intermediary between the worlds? It is not in my nature to sort out these complex distinctions.

What I want to convey are my own experiences of being taken over, seized, wrestled with all night long. I want to convey how a figure can emerge out of a reverie, a dream, a fleeting memory, a difficult emotion. If you let that figure speak you will learn what you didn't know you knew, you will make sense of memories, or be filled with the urgency of a poem that demands to be written. The muse makes weird things happen, excites your passions, moves

---

2 Angeles Arrien, *The Nine Muses*, pp. 6-7.

3 C.M. Bowra, *Greek Lyric Poetry*, p. 29.

4 Sappho, translated by Mary Barnard, fragment # 25.

5 C.G. Jung, *Mysterium*. CW Vol. 14, p. 497. (CW refers throughout to *The Collected Works of C.G. Jung*.)

6 Jung, *Memories, Dreams, Reflections*, pp. 44-45.

your soul, lifts the veil on other realities, can send you into agony or ecstasy, depending on her mood.

When the muse appears, as Robert Graves says, your "hair stands on end . . . eyes water,"[7] you feel turned on, charged with erotic feeling. Colors are bright, images clearly faceted, words come as music to your inner ear. Do you know Her in yourself? Sometimes She is like a tug from a dreamy eyed child who'd rather wander in the woods, make-believe all kinds of wondrous things, than go through your to-do list. Sometimes She's a bitch on wheels. My muse has not, like Dante's Beatrice, *waited* patiently for me and lifted me to the heavens. She's been a nudge, a nag, an intruder, a banshee—flying into a screaming rage if She does not get the time She considers Her due.

I write of nine manifestations in which the muse has visited me, stirred up creative ferment, found me my voice as a poet, filled me with stories of ghosts, mysteries, erotic teachings, the old religion. In my experience the muse can be an inner figure, a fleeting memory from early childhood, an ancestor, a figure from myth or from a dream, an image of a culture, a dead poet, or a ghost from one's personal past.

The muse has come to me in the form of the "Sister from Below," the inner poet who has spoken for the soul since language began. She has been trying to get my attention all my life. A visit to Florence, where I lived for a year as a young child, filled me with yearning for my first muse, a nursemaid whom I longed to meet again. The muse leapt into my reverie out of a poem I was working on, in the form of Eurydice, a figure from a famous myth. Eurydice was the beloved wife of the poet Orpheus. When she died he went down into the underworld to bring her back. Many poems have been written from his point of view. When Eurydice visited me, her story was a different and surprising one.

My muse came as the ghost of a grandmother I never met, who died in the Shoah, and had unfinished business with me. The muse visited me in the form of Old Mother India, whose culture I visited as a young woman. She cracked open my Western mind, and flooded me with Her many gods and goddesses. She came to me as Sappho, the great lyric poet of the ancient world, who entered my imagination with a lovely midlife fantasy. In a dream She appeared as Helena, a root vegetable, dressed in a flowery summer dress, and kept appearing again and again on a journey I took to the ancient land

---

7 Graves, *The White Goddess*, p. 24.

of Thrace, now called Bulgaria. She came as "Die Ur Naomi," an old woman from the biblical story for which I was named, who insisted on telling me Her version of the Book of Ruth. And in the end, to my surprise, the muse came in the form of a man, a poet I'd loved in my youth, long dead.

There are many, Robert Graves among them, who would say that the muse is always female. At the beginning of my journey I would have agreed with him. But I was taken to places and given experiences that showed me another aspect of the muse. Graves, after all, writes as a man, a male poet. We know much of the male experience of the muse. We know how Orpheus risked everything to find his Eurydice. We know how that one glimpse of Beatrice illuminated Dante's life and became the wellspring for the Divine Comedy. We know how the "dark lady" wanders through the sonnets of Shakespeare. But what of a woman poet? Since the days of Enheduanna and Sappho, what do we know of her experience of the muse? Perhaps, as women learn more about the white goddess in our history, and in ourselves, as we stand on the grounds of our own deep female nature, we will be freed to experience the muse as male, as well as female.

The *Sister from Below* is the story of my relationship to the muse. I imagine this book shaped as a mandala, a flower. Each petal comes from a different experience in my life. Each begins in a different place. But each connects at the core to the central theme of the muse. Or, I imagine this book as a necklace made of beads, each a different color and shape, but all held together by that common thread—the forms of the muse that have been revealed to me.

I invite you to enter my inner world, peopled by the figures of my imagination, to go with me on inner and outer journeys, to experience with me the tumult of creativity and weird visitations. I hope you will be inspired to listen to your own muse, in whatever forms She (or He) comes to you.

The Argument

She . . . she Who she?
—Judy Grahn[8]

The Woman You're Not

She's been persistent. We've argued for years. We don't have the same goals for my life. I thought She was a distraction, a frivolity. Who has time for poetry when the world is such a perilous place? And anyway, She was making a shambles of my life. She'd blast me with intense images, or send me careening off, intoxicated with the power of some word; I'd not be heard from for hours. The dishes wouldn't get done. The children's dinner wouldn't get cooked. I had to send Her into exile.

That was a long time ago. I was a single mother with young children. She'd come along in the form of ecstasy, of poetry, saying She'd always been there, that She was the true stuff of life. She broke up my first marriage. That was necessary. I had married too young and for all the wrong reasons. I had lost contact with the one I was, one I'd known from time to time, in childhood. Imprisoned in a false version of myself, She was a wild wind, or an earthquake, that knocked that prison down.

But, when She took over I couldn't get anything done. I needed to earn a living, to make a practical connection to the world, not wander about for days in her underworlds. She was a bad influence. I stopped listening to her, went back to school, became a psychotherapist and eventually a Jungian analyst. I had meaningful work now, an office, where I was useful.

But She refused to stay away, though I tried to fend her off. She was bad for my mental health, so I drew a line in the sand: psychology on one side, the safe side, the good side; poetry on the other side, dangerous, wild.

Nonsense! She cried, and did a fierce dance in the sand, obliterating my line, *poetry and psychology are fruits of the same world tree. This tree,* She told me, *has its roots in the eternal underworld, where dead souls wander and dark gods reign; its branches reach up into the realm of flight, into spiritual imagina-*

---

8 Judy Grahn, *She Who*, p. 5.

tion. *Its fruits offer those who taste them what the Hindus call the "rasas" of life, life's juices, life's essential emotions. Long before psychology became its own branch of the world tree, poetry was the medium through which psyche knew herself, felt herself, tasted the fruit of the tree.*

Slow down, I say. You're blasting me with those big images again. I'm trying to keep my feet on the ground of everyday life.

So you should. But you can't be grounded if you don't know the ground you're standing on. Poetry is psyche's first language, everyone's first language. It begins in our ancestral need to talk to the gods, to invoke, to evoke, to chant, to pray, to use the human voice to make a bridge between the inner and the outer realms. Those who want to know their roots, who want access to a creativity that comes from the depths, need to listen to me. I go by many names, I wear many faces. I am the poem that appears in the dark, when the fire has been lit. I am the trance that comes over you when you see the moon. I am that ineffable feeling you have when a boundary between the worlds has been crossed. I make my way through your throat to your tongue:

the woman you're not

is sure of her great
breasted body
mermaid to this one
siren to that she knows
        where to put her feet knows
                 each step
                     of the dance
       and her voice from the deep
                of her belly
    how she flings it about
                like her long fiery hair
    her laugh that collides
              with the stars

fear never touches her
whose dreams rise up like sap
       and any man who knows her knows her teeth
           and the back of her hand

she grows crystals
                    at the bottom of your garden
wears purple silk and lavender chiffon
travels in a green and yellow covered wagon
                    drawn by seven giraffes

this morning in a dream she's handed you an image
              under glass a bale of hay
                    in a field of darkness

                                    burning[9]

Hey! That's my poem!

*Not exactly. It's **my** poem I gave it to you. It is my own wild harvest of your dreams.*

I'm grateful for the poem. It's a gift. But I'm not the woman who has no fear. What's the purpose of leaping about between the worlds when the country is at war, when not so long ago towers fell, when every day we hear terrible news?

I've been singing of war since poetry began. Remember Homer? Remember the Trojan war? I sang of those towers that fell. I sang of those many who died.

Well I'm no Homer, and I can't be leaping all over creation when work is calling.

I am the source of the creative in you, in everyone. When you forget me you feel dead inside, lost, out of touch with your center. I am the tree of life whose roots go down into childhood, into the realm of the ancestors, into the dream world, into the myths that shape you, into the secret power of the very language you use. The poet Denise Levertov, who responded in her work to the war and terror of her times, describes language as a "form of life and a common resource to be cherished and served as we should serve and cherish earth and its water, animal and vegetable life, and each other."[10] But so many are cut off from the sacred roots of language—"mere words," they say, as though words don't have their magical roots in that treasure trove of ancestral imagery, the collective unconscious. You need me to do your work.

---

9   Lowinsky, *crimes of the dreamer*, p. 58.
10   Denise Levertov, 'Origins of a Poem,' in Donald Hall, *Claims for Poetry*, p. 262.

I resist Her. She is so pushy. I'm not sure what you're trying to say here. The work of the poet is to make a poem. I can't be making poetry all the time. I have to make a living!

You'll make a better living if you keep me with you, see through my eyes, hear through my ears. You'll hear the mythic story behind the one you're being told; you'll see the images in the roots of the words, catch the spirit that moves behind them. Invoke me wherever you go, whatever you do. When you are washing dishes gaze out the window and see the light in the plum tree, recognize that it is blooming. In the grocery store see the beauty in the piles of red and green apples, oranges, grapes and bananas in the produce aisle. Children see like this all the time. The poet Robert Duncan understood this. He wrote:

> The roots and depths of mature thought, its creative sources, lie in childhood or even "childish" things I have not put away but taken as enduring realities of my being....The child hears the heart of speech, the emotional and illustrative creation.... Like the poet, the child dwells not in the literal meanings of words but in the spirit that moves behind them.[11]

He also said this beautifully in a poem:

From the beginning, color
and light, my nurse; sounding waves
and air, my nurse; animal presences
my nurse; Night, my nurse.[12]

But I am no longer a child. I am trying to be a responsible adult. If I get all involved in the spirit that moves behind words I'll never get anything done.

If you don't pay attention to the spirit behind words you'll lose contact with me, and with your deeper life. You have no life without me. Don't split me off. You'll feel deadened. You need me with you always. When you are moved, when affect and image come together, there I am. When you breathe deeply, and know what you are feeling, there I am. When a fragment of dream comes back and invades your daylight mind, there I am. When you're turned on, excited, there I am. I am the poet in you, your Sister from Below, the voice of what is deep in you, wild in you, erotic in you.

---

11   Robert Duncan, *Fictive Certainties*, p. 6.
12   Robert Duncan, *Ground Work: Before the War.* p. 96.

Poetry Head

She *is* convincing. She claims that in the beginning of my life, She, the poet in me, was ascendant. She thought I'd devote my life to Her, which was, She is convinced, Her due. It hasn't worked out that way. I've told Her, time and again, that I've done it all for Her. Neither one of us would have survived had I not. This argument does not impress Her. After a few years spent in a major pout she began staging Her comeback, guerilla warrior style, infiltrating the landscape of my consciousness, raiding my time and attention.

How has She managed this coup—the successful invasion of the life of a harried professional with children, stepchildren, grandchildren, a husband? Very simply: by inserting Herself into everything I think, write, teach, do. In every aspect of my life I hear Her voice, giving me *Her* rendition of my experience. She wants to slow everything down, to get to the heart of every feeling, the meaning under the meaning, the image within the word.

I finally surrender, even in my work as an analyst. She says there is no creativity, no transformation possible without her help. She puts her ear to the ground of the language I hear in my consulting room, helping me hear "the heart of speech" or dark intuitions reaching for "visible form." I find that her impulse to get to the bottom of an image, a feeling, a presence in the room, to give voice to its deepest nature, supports my analytic concerns. You'd think She'd feel valued. You'd think our long argument would be over. But it's not enough for her. She's like the fisherman's wife in the fairy tale, who keeps wanting *more*. Next She told me she was tired of hearing the poetry in other people's voices; She wanted time for Her own poetry. But I didn't have that kind of time; when I put time in Her hands She takes forever, dreaming, dawdling, working for hours on a single line.

That was when She began intruding on my personal life. My husband Dan can attest to this. She began invading our vacations, putting me into a trance state which She calls "poetry head." Dan could barely have a conversation with me, so much was I being called inward to listen to Her. She'd squeeze at least one poem out of every trip. She got bolder. She began sneaking her poems into my prose pieces for journals.

I struck a deal with Her. I made a time and place to listen to her everyday. And every week I gave Her a full day or two for poetry. I found I was happiest when a poem was cooking in the back of my mind. It brought luster to my everyday pursuits, and what the day brought, would often bring new light to the poem. Again I thanked Her, told Her she was right. Again She wanted more.

What more do you want? I cry, my soul?

Get off it! says She. *I **am** your soul and you know it. I want a legitimate place in your life. If I had a real voice in your calling I wouldn't have to be sneaky, wouldn't have to push my way in where I'm not wanted. If I could take the driver's seat, I wouldn't be a back seat driver!*

She's getting shrill. Give some parts of yourself an inch and they take a mile! I don't understand what more you could ask of me, I tell her. I've given you time. We now devote certain hours every week to writing. I give you attention. We read poetry, subscribe to poetry magazines. What more do you want?

It's very simple. When you give a talk I want it to be in my voice. When you write a book, I want to be its author. I want to come out of the closet. I want to be taken seriously.

What if you embarrass me?

What if I do? You embarrass me *all the time! You insist, for example, on separating poetry and prose. Why should they have to go off and live in different books? Why shouldn't they cohabit the same pages? They are different ways into the same experience. Prose tells the story, and poetry breaks into song. Prose gives the background, the landscape, and poetry fills in the myth, the unseen, the divine and demonic presences. For example that poem called "Initiate" that I handed you after you'd been reading the poet H.D. It's in her style and it came out so clearly you needed to make few revisions.*

White Temple cut in gray rock
I have washed the stone floors
I have put the full blown
white peony
in amber glass
only Hecate knows the dark center

Through an arched window
blood red madrone stains the rocky slope
Snake is sacred here
also mongoose

I await you
daughter of Isis

lover of the blood lord
sister of the frenzied one

climb the mountain in your bare feet
bring me your mouth and young breasts
white cave is the place I have prepared for you
hot flame of female word[13]

I see. You want payback for giving me that poem without a struggle. I get it now, the poem is about you and me. I am the initiate in whom you have prepared a place for the "hot flame of female word." So what do you propose we write about in our white cave?

The creativity I bring to those who make a place for me in their lives, my many voices, as they are revealed to you, for "I am large, I contain multitudes!"[14]

Hey! You stole that line from Whitman!

Of course. Poetry is, among other things, stealing. We borrow, join, rephrase our influences consciously or unconsciously. As Rilke said: "Ultimately there is only one poet, that infinite one who makes himself felt, here and there through the ages, in a mind that can surrender to him."[15] *I want this to be a book about the one poet as I come through your particular life. My voice comes to you from myth, from dream, from journeys, from gods that have appeared to you, poems that have passed through you. I am your guide from below, from within.*

Wait a minute. I didn't spend all those years getting my roots into the ground of my real life, in order to be annihilated by you in my own book!

I'm not trying to annihilate you. I keep telling you, I have no life without you. The book I envision is entirely your book, your story. Much of it is in your voice, informed by how I know your life. I just make occasional appearances in various guises. I am your muse, your good angel. You are the flesh in which I manifest. I'll take you all over the world, through the millennia. I will give you many different experiences of me. You're a woman on a journey to gather up the pieces of your life, the myths that have shaped you, the eternal figures that visit you, and I will be your guide.

I don't have a problem being the woman on a journey, guided by you, for I am that. But I also want to speak as the woman I am.

---

13 Lowinsky, *red clay is talking*, p. 121.
14 Walt Whitman, *Leaves of Grass*, p. 113.
15 William H. Gass, *Reading Rilke*, p. 183.

You and your lived life are the ground I spring from. I would have no exis-tence without you. So your perspective, your memories, your life experience are essential here. This is a dialogue.

And so it is that I and my "Sister from Below," in her many shape-shifting forms, got together to write this book.

When the Sister Gets Her Way

I always knew that I was two persons. One was the son of my parents . . . The other was . . . old . . . remote from the world of men, but close to nature, the earth, the sun, the moon . . . and above all close to the night, to dreams, and to whatever "God" worked directly in him . . .

—C.G. Jung[16]

A Soul at the White Heat

As I'm sure you've gathered, it's been a long struggle for me to find my way into my above ground sister's life. Who are we to one another, we two parts of this one person? She is what Jung called the #1 part of the personality, the ego, the reality principle, the payer of bills, the listener to news. She belongs to this time. I am #2, what Jungians call the Self, the mysterious center of the personality, the vastness of the unconscious. I belong to all time.

She doesn't realize it, my daylight other, but I am grateful for her green growth in the practical air, her roots in a particular time and place, the sunshine and rain realities of work and relationships. They feed us both. Without that, and more years than she'd want me to say of Jungian analysis, neither one of us would have survived. Jung wrote of the poet, in this case Rilke, that he "doesn't have what it takes to make a man complete: body, weight, shadow."[17] Without my above-ground sister, I would not have the body, weight and shadow to make myself complete. I would be insubstantial.

She needs me to make her life complete as well, my above-ground sister. I love the analytic work she puts me to, deeply hearing the voices of others. But she also needs me to deeply hear herself, or she will dry up, lose contact with the wellsprings of her soul. When she gets caught up in planning dinners, worrying about money, dealing with politics, answering e-mail, she forgets who she really is.

It's been a lifelong challenge for me, getting her attention. She knew me when she was a child, but hid me from her parents who would have called me "fresh" and sent her to her room. Do you remember, my above-ground sister, when you

---

16 Jung, *Memories, Dreams, Reflections*, pp. 44-45.
17 Jung, *Letters*, Vol. 2, p. 382.

*were eight and your family moved from the cityscape of New York, to the coun-
try world of Princeton, New Jersey—I was released from the prison of streets
and pavements. That was a good time for me. I spent many hours with you in
the woods being the wild horse of your imagination. You knew me in the oak
tree where you'd sit for hours, reading, daydreaming.*

I do remember. To this day it's easier to connect with you in the woods,
or by a body of water. To this day it's easier to find you when I'm alone. My
family was so haunted, there were so many ghosts, I was afraid if I listened to
you some terrible trouble would get stirred up.

*I understand that. Your parents were German Jews who got out of Europe
just in time, leaving behind so many who died in concentration camps, including your own father's parents. With ghosts like that it's hard for a girl to feel her
own life matters. Time and again you've said to me, you could have been Anne
Frank, dead at thirteen. Why weren't you, you wondered. Why did you get to
live?*

*And when your body changed, when you developed breasts, and the time of
your blood began, you did what so many young women do, you squelched me,
except for the occasional impassioned English paper, or poem I gave you that
was fierce enough to crack your resistance. I did not abandon you. I visited,
even when I wasn't welcome. Do you remember that evening, you were about
fourteen, when I stood behind your right shoulder watching the day fade away,
the bay darken, fog flow in over the Golden Gate?*

I do remember. There was that strange sensation of seeing one world with
the eyes of another. Here I was in California which so recently had been a
mythic land when I was still in New York and New Jersey. I'd heard stories
about fruit trees in people's backyards, tall palms, bridges, a glowing bay. It
had sounded like magic. Now, here I was, looking at it all. My parents were
having a party and I was hiding out with you in my darkening bedroom.
Remember the sounds: laughter, exclamations, voices being witty. It was
Berkeley, 1957. Eisenhower was President; change was just beginning to happen. Eisenhower had sent troops to Little Rock to force desegregation. The
Russians had launched Sputnik. My father's colleagues from the University
would be talking about all that.

*Yes, but what they wouldn't be talking about, which was of great conse-
quence to you, was that Alan Ginsberg had come to Berkeley, Howl had been
published, you had read it and your mind had been blown. You liked to put on*

black stockings and hang out at the "Cafe Mediterranean" on Telegraph Avenue, hoping you looked like a beat poet.

Right. That was where I would have preferred to be, but I had claimed too much homework so I could get out of serving food at the party. My mother would be doing it, offering Ritz crackers with cream cheese, a circle of salami and a piece of parsley on each one. Also her sour cream and spinach dip. I know. I had helped assemble them. From my bedroom I could see the animated room below—signifying eyes, opening and closing mouths, elegant clothes. I could smell the women's perfumes, and my father's vivid European splash of 4711 Eau de Cologne. Smoke. People still smoked in those days. It was considered elegant to keep a container of cigarettes on the coffee table. Hard to imagine that the whole living room world was oblivious to the glory before me: the sky, the golden orb of the sun setting into a bank of fog streaming into the bay, sending fingers of white glowing across the darkening waters.

I was telling you a secret, revealing a mystery: there are always at least two worlds. Poetry comes in the dance between them, between the people in the living room and the angels who walked across the bay on fog fingers. I was whispering a poem to you, about all this, but you didn't write it down. You just kept looking out the window, filled with inexplicable longing. I did my best to feed you. I gave you Walt Whitman:

"Stop this day and night with me and you shall possess the origin of all poems"[18]

I gave you Emily Dickinson:

The soul selects her own Society—
Then—shuts the Door—[19]

I loved Whitman. I wanted to lie in the grass with him and invite my soul. Emily Dickinson took my breath away:

"Dare you see a Soul at the White Heat?"[20]

She was a mystic, a priestess. When I read her the other world was touched, another dimension opened. I wanted to go there, to live where Emily lived,

---

18   Walt Whitman, *Leaves of Grass*, p. 35.
19   Emily Dickinson, *The Complete Poems*, p. 143.
20   Dickinson, p. 173

to be in that intensity in which the most ordinary things, a butterfly, a bee, an anvil, connect one to eternity. I longed to know the White Heat. And yet I feared it. For I also longed for the red fire, the common fire. I did not really want a life like Emily Dickinson's, in her white dress, wandering the confines of her father's house and garden, knowing the body heat of no lover, knowing the sweet smell of no babies in her arms. As a young girl I had been able to go past "the houses—past the headlands—into Deep Eternity"[21] with Dickinson. But now I had new breasts, strange yearnings. I had other plans besides listening to you. I wanted love. My ghosts demanded babies.

The Red Fire

Your two worlds were pulling me apart, threatening to rip open the sky, to sever my heart from my body. You were so wild and cruel, filling me with grandiose visions. I couldn't handle your poets and angels. Trying to catch the poems you were giving me on paper seemed like leaping into the ocean. I was so young, so unformed, so deeply afraid of life. I wanted security. Soon I was off, entwined around my young man, married at eighteen, pregnant at nineteen.

I thought I had successfully fought you off and found my own little life. I had no idea that I was possessed by ghosts until you explained it all to me years later in a poem. You came to me in the form of Hera, the goddess of marriage, and told me my story from the vantage of the eternal forms. It's called "Hera Reflects on the Anniversary of a Long Ago Dissolved First Marriage."[22] I used an epigraph from H.D. which summed it up neatly: "I will rise/ from my troth with the dead."

> White narcissus
> pale blue
> forget-me-nots
> composed your wedding
> bouquet
>
> There were more dead
> than living

---

21 Dickinson, p. 39.
22 Lowinsky, *red clay is talking*, pp. 38-42.

among the guests
and of the gods
I was the only one
who knew
a woman's
way

Demeter did not
come
she sat on her rock
she'd had enough
of daughters
in the underworld

I took the form of
the shadow cast
by a silver vase of lilies
on the altar
I took the form of
the ache
between your shoulder blades
the unholy
ferment
in your brain

Who else was there?
Besides the puffed up rabbi
the too young groom
the quarreling parents
on both sides
the only surviving
grandmother and those armies
of European dead
on their way
to Jerusalem?

Zeus came
on the groom's side
he sees it as his job
to kiss the bride
and organize her mind
into a small
neat package

lavender sachet
to fit inside a drawer
on the right side
of her husband's
busy brain

I won't allow it
I took the form of
snakes
I mixed the blood
and the milk
I waited for you
in the apple tree—

Aphrodite did not
come
her laugh
was not heard
all day
all night
her gold did not
shine
she took off
to the backside of the moon
that was her howling
you heard
her keening
her keeping wild company
with Lilith

Hestia sent you
no gift
Artemis
gave you
not even
a backward glance
having caught
not a glimpse
of you
in her woods
since you were ten

And I who received

no sacrifice
no offering
no song
no prayer
took the form of
that cold shadow
on your wedding night
no wild thing bloomed
no flower flowered
no blood to show
That was no marriage
that was a wooly blanket for cold feet
a pillow for a pain in the neck
a menstrual cave
for all those
European ghosts
fresh out
of the ovens
fresh out of
mass graves
they had

no stones
to lay down their heads
no baskets
for their bones
no grounds
for their roots
they spilled over
oceans
invading
demanding
new born
baby bodies

Demeter changed
her mind
she came
to live with you
every evening
she swept the ghosts
out of your house
every night

before the dawn
they came back
by the time the children
went down
for their naps
ghosts had
torn you
into pieces
in the midday sun

I took the form of
the shadow
that shielded you
the shadow
that froze you
for seven years
I had other plans for you
So did Aphrodite
So did Lilith

Even Hestia knew
her time would come
But it was Artemis
who built a bark for you
out of the wild papyrus
down by the river
in the dark
of a new moon
she who knew
the wild ways
the sacred ways
showed you
showed you
your craft

Can Poetry Change Such a World?

*I don't care whether dinner gets cooked or whether you study for exams. But I
have no life unless you pay attention to me, bring me into your ordinary flesh
and blood experience. Even in those years when, as Hera says in the poem, I*

shielded you and kept you frozen, I visited you, I kept you company. How do I get to those who have lost contact with me? I have my ways: dreams, fantasies, mountains, bodies of water, music, poetry.

There are those who would say a person should meet you in a temple, or a church.

Some do. But too often they get a tame, second hand version of me, not their own wild alive experience. Remember how suffocated you felt in temple as a teenager? How hungry you were for an immediate experience of soul?

I do. The service seemed so set. The energy was mostly social, about being seen and seeing others. The rabbi rushed past the minute of silence as though it was dangerous.

It is dangerous, that quiet moment that allows me in. You never know what I'm going to say, or do. That's why you've been so ambivalent about me. In the temple you longed for me. In your everyday life you shunned me. But I found my way back to you at the university, via poetry. You were trading babysitting with several other women so you could have time to attend classes. It's a strange thing about universities, they so easily press the life out of ideas, and yet they are a great breeding ground for me and mine. There I would waylay you, away from the baby and the house, remind you of the pleasures of beautiful language, the power it has to invoke other states of being. I filled you with the voice of T.S. Eliot, do you remember?

> The silent sister veiled in white and blue
> Between the yews, behind the garden god…[23]

I do remember. I was enchanted by "*Ash Wednesday.*" How could words do this amazing thing, transport one to another realm where a veiled sister prayed, where the bones of one who had been eaten by three white leopards spoke to the Lady and to me, of devotions, of mysteries, of a deeper life? I longed for that life, yet feared it would devour me, rip me to pieces, as the poem's narrator had been, as my own people had been, as I feared you would devour me.

When I learned that this magician of language, who could shift my consciousness into realms which were at once mythic and ordinary, familiar as snatches of conversation heard on a bus, and mystical as the writings of saints, was an anti-Semite and a misogynist, who kept company with that

---

23 T.S. Eliot, *The Complete Poems and Plays*, p. 64.

famous fascist Ezra Pound, I decided you were not to be trusted. How could I, with the crematoria of Europe so recently behind my people, let myself be transported by such a poet?

I do not claim to be wise about human affairs. That's why I need you, to humanize me. And those who devote themselves to me, who are filled with my wild flow through the millennia and can leap about from the ancients to today, are prone to confuse their own blind spots, their "suburban prejudices" as Pound came to call his anti-Semitism late in his life, with the great truths.

So, now my work was cut out for me. I had to find a way to ignite your love for me, for poetry, while you had your babies and lived your ordinary life, in a way that did not clash with your young woman early 1960s politics. I was rather clever, how I achieved this. Do you remember?

I remember . . . how did you come up with that short story that took me over? It was called *"Die Heimkehr des Vergil's"* (Virgil Comes Home), and written by the 20th century Austrian poet and novelist Herman Broch. I have no memory of how it found me, for that's how it feels. But the story lit an image in my heart, which has stayed lit ever since, an image that allowed me to understand the function of poetry. You leapt upon the convenient vehicle of a task I had to do for the University, a Senior Honors Thesis.

I don't recall how I persuaded my professor that a German short story was an appropriate topic for an English Department thesis. I translated the story from the German myself. Broch, though not Jewish, was a political activist who was jailed by the Nazis in 1935. While in jail, the image of a dying Virgil came to Broch. The image that burnt itself into my consciousness then is contained in the following passage from Broch's story:

> With what can one respond to all the blood, the many slaughters, and all the torment? With poetry? Isn't poetry too little and yet too much? Can poetry change such a world? Virgil, the singer, dozed, he was suspended... like the strings of a lyre, yet he himself was the lyre and he awaited the hand which would take hold of his heart...longingly he awaited this hand because when his heart resounded, it would no longer burn. And behold, as he lay there, dozing...and feeling how the noonday night ebbed away...so that the Nymphs, like shepherds, had long ago disappeared into the darkness... Virgil spread out his arms, as though he had to make himself into a cross and enter the landscape of evening forever, for he heard anew the angel who said: "Grow little child, grow. Resound and lead, lead through time, portend into eternity."[24]

24 Herman Broch, *Die Heimkehr des Vergil*, pp. 45-55. My unpublished translation.

I was so excited when I found that short story; I loved translating it. Something came to life in me, feeling the connection between my time and Virgil's. It helped with my struggle, to justify my love of poetry. Broch knew the cruelty of the time into which I was born. He put into Virgil's mouth my own lament: "With what can one respond to all the blood, the many slaughters, and all the torment? With poetry? Isn't poetry too little and yet too much? Can poetry change such a world?"

Poetry seemed a luxury, a foolishness, in a world where six million Jews had been murdered, where a hundred years after the end of slavery there was still segregation, men were still being lynched. I accused myself of not being a serious person. I should be picketing and demonstrating, making an effort to change the world. Broch's image of Virgil's death bed wrestlings gave voice to my own struggles, and then transformed them into the amazing image of the poet as musical instrument. It dawned on me that poetry might not be only about what one knew consciously. One might also serve by being receptive, by letting oneself be played.

What was burned into my consciousness was the image of the angel coming to Virgil, and quoting to him from his own poetry, prophesying the coming of the new god, Christ. Broch was expanding on a medieval tradition that regarded Virgil's Fourth Eclogue as a prophesy of the birth of Christ. Virgil's liminal role in the time of changing myths was a powerful image to the medieval mind. In *The Divine Comedy*, Dante's guide to the Christian universe is Virgil. Dante entreats him: "Poet, by that god to you unknown, lead me."[25] What was burned into the back of my mind was the image of the poet as an instrument being played by an unknown god.

This very image came to Robert Duncan: "And he/ as if moving his hands across taut/ strings of me..."[26] Through Broch and Duncan you gave me a glimpse of your truth, that poetry has a prophetic function, that I was living in a time of changing myths, and the new gods are playing their poets like instruments.

---

25 Dante, *Inferno*, p. 5.
26 Robert Duncan, *Ground Work: Before the War*, p. 123.

Self Portrait of My Grandmother

So I had you reading poetry, thinking about poetry, but not yet writing it. I thought my chance had come when you were pregnant with your second child. You decided you'd had enough of the University, it dulled your spirit, put you into a torpor of footnotes and abstractions. You told me you were ready to make space for your own wild voice, strange imagery, strong feeling. You rented a room and tried to find me. I was there, in the tree outside the window, in the sky, in the breath that went in and out of your body. But you could not find me. You were so constricted, trying to fit into a narrow version of yourself, not offend anyone, even in writing you might never show them. So you stayed on surfaces. Had you plunged into your real depths you might have found out you were in the wrong marriage, living a pretend life.

Don't ask to speak to your angel, your wild nature, unless you're ready to face some truths about yourself. If there are things you don't want to think, places in your psyche you don't want to go, avoid me. Worlds shatter when I appear. I can take the form of earthquake and flood.

It's a terrible feeling, staring at a blank page with nothing true, nothing fierce coming at you. Just vague ideas. Clanking gears. Critical voices. Nothing leaps at you from behind the bushes. Nothing wrestles with you from the other side.

I was pregnant. It was such a powerful experience. I should have been able to write something that would give female voice to this profound human experience, for what woman, in those days, had written of it? I wasn't able to complete that book until the child I bore was a young woman! I had a lot of life to live before I could handle you.

You had to risk everything, you had to leave a marriage, your so called security, your home, money, children's welfare. In a dream I was an earthquake, or maybe a great wind, and I knocked down the fortress in which you lived. It wasn't your personal castle. It was the fortress of convention, of the collective culture that knew nothing of your individuality.

It's a difficult business, calling a mortal, waking a person up. It happens only in extreme situations, when things seem to be falling apart. I finally got through to you, when you were a single mother, vulnerable and confused, in a dream about your grandmother's death. Do you remember?

Yes, she was the only grandparent I'd known, Oma. My grandfather, her husband, had died when I was just a baby. And my father's parents died in concentration camps in Europe. We had a special tie; I was the first grandchild in the new world, the new life after all the chaos and the losses. She was a painter. And when tragedy struck her as it often did, she painted—portraits, landscapes, still lifes. There was a quality of light that shone through her work, and a complexity of shadow. She taught me that a woman could live a full woman's life, have children, a marriage, and also be an artist.

Toward the end of her long life, when I returned to the states after two years in India, I saw her in a nursing home. She was demented, crazy with ghosts and demons. I could not tell if she recognized me. Soon after she died and I received her ashes in a strange little box. In the dream I saw her dying. It was a long powerful process, like a labor, and the dream opened me up to poetry like a birth, insisted I write it down. It was a message from her; I had to take up my art.

It was from her, but also from me. I was claiming you through her. It worked. Finally you began to listen to me, finally you began to write. That was your first real poem. And you put it in your poetry collection, though it was written 30 years before much of your work, because you knew it was the poem that called you to the craft.

Self Portrait of My Grandmother

When my grandmother lay dying in a strange home
I came from far away to see
her sinking like a shadow into white sheets.
          Oma—do you know who I am?

They kept her in a flourescent room.
For color they allowed
the portrait of her husband—flushed pink with heart disease—
Opa—whom I never knew.

I saw her eyes go dark and inward
the beginning of death tightens within her
thrashing
she asks for no help
just grunts like an idiot child

Her eyes start out
of her head
Her body arches
   higher higher
   bellowing grunting
      higher higher
     her tongue reaches out for the last
         sweet taste of the air

Death labor drops her
       limp
      back on the bed

    Oma—look and see me
When I was a child you painted
it was forbidden to watch
but I crept over the grass once, quietly
to see how you stared at a tree
your eyes went hard, your face looked cruel,
and I was afraid of you—
My gracious lady—
when I sat on your lap
how softly the skin hung
from your withering arms
your eyes, smiling at me
were strangely violet.

Once you painted me fat and trembling
now you are dying
They have come to change your diapers, and I am ashamed.
     Listen Oma: I'll tell them!
I'll tell them you painted tigers
and flowers and babies and trees
and you could make a shadow
outgrow the thing that threw it
so intricate, so subtle you drew it
I'll tell them you bore six children and buried three
outliving the six million and all the generation
that you knew
a refugee Jew
But they say you must take your medicine now
    Oma—when will this death be over?

For a moment you smile—your eyes are aglow

who is it you see? Your sister? Your brother?
Your mother who died when you were very young?
Your two sons, insanely
dead in the snow?
perhaps, you see me?

Your eyes go dark and inward and I leave
Your bellows pursue me
                    Oma—I left you
to them
you were a troublesome old lady
who bit her nurses
spat out her medicine
and was afraid to die

For myself
I keep the portrait:
you
painting yourself
painting
in a mirror[27]

Sister of the Frenzied One

That poem was like a tunnel blasted through rock. It opened me to you, filled me with archetypal energy and a frenzy to write. You've said a lot about the struggle you've had to get through to me. But what of the struggle I've had to contain you, to channel you, to bring you down to earth so I could make something of you? Sometimes you've given me a poem that is all of a piece, like "Self Portrait of My Grandmother," but that is rare. Most of the time I feel a poem wanting to form as a glimmering, a piece of light in a whirlwind, or a phrase that fills me with energy but gives me no clarity. I get agitated, but nothing comes. This is no ecstasy.

You dance around me, flaunting your veils, passing them over my hands, for a moment, then out of my grasp. A glimpse of an image, something that glows and is full of light, but I can't quite see it, a snatch of your music, brief pulse of your rhythm and then you're gone. And I am wandering around

---

27 Lowinsky, *red clay is talking*, pp. 20-22.

the house feeling lost. I make a cup of tea. I wash some dishes. If I am lucky you give me another glimpse. This can go on for days. I wake up in the night listening for more.

In those early days of writing, when those huge blasts of unformed energy passed through me, I was not strong enough to contain them. I'd end up on the floor, or eating tablespoons full of peanut butter, as though that would protect me from the intensity of what you were pouring through me.

You had not yet learned to sort out the voices within you. You did not know how to distinguish the voice of the poem, my voice, from the critic who says "this is no good, this is going nowhere" or from the voice that says "make a name for yourself" or "where are you going to publish this?" You confused external acclaim with my blessing. You couldn't tolerate rejections. You were a frenzy of unfulfilled emotional needs which you poured into me. I can't give you human love or recognition. You needed to go out and find those in other realms. And you needed to learn that destruction and chaos are natural phenomena, not just the product of human evil.

You were experiencing what the alchemists call a "nigredo," a dark night of the soul. That is not necessarily a bad thing. It's how old rigidities and patterns get broken down so new life can spring up. It was when you first discovered the myth of Inanna that your experience with me began to make sense. Do you remember?

Yes, when I first got wind of Inanna's myth, reading the work of Joseph Henderson:

> One of (the) great mythologems is told in the story of the Sumerian goddess Inanna . . . She descended to the underworld, the land of No Return, experienced death, and achieved the impossible return to life again . . . Here the journey is a kind of mystery in which Inanna accomplished the quest of herself and emerges as one reborn from a symbolic sacrifice and death.[28]

I began to see that the underworld was not just a place to die, or to wander disembodied, cut off from one's creative source. It *is* the creative source, where the roots of life, literally in plants and trees, metaphorically in the descent to one's depths, begin. I understood life differently when contemplating the myth of the goddess who descends to the underworld to meet her dark sister. I could better understand what was happening to me when I realized that a woman, Enheduanna, the high priestess of the moon god at Ur and the first poet of record, wrote this great mythic poem over five thousand years

28 Joseph Henderson and Maud Oakes, *The Wisdom of the Serpent*, pp. 15-16.

ago. The goddess is stripped of her finery, her lapis beads, her breast plate, her power. Betty de Shong Meador has made a magnificent translation of the poem:

> when she enters the seventh gate
> someone unwraps
> the Lady's royal robe
> someone strips away
> the Ladyship royal robe
>
> she is naked now and bowed low

WHAT IS THIS

> silent Inanna
> sacred customs
> must be fulfilled
>
> do not open your mouth
> against this rite[29]

Inanna enters the underworld, is caught in the "eye of death" of her underworld sister, and is hung on a meat hook, turning green. That image is written into my very being.

Of course it is. You knew that meat hook. You had done time on it; you almost died on it. You thought it was my fault, that poetry could not sustain your life, that I was bad for you and had made you sick. You were partly right. You needed to find your single ordinary life, your roots in the earth, and not be over identified with me. I am dangerous to those who don't have a strong hold on their own life. The Jungians call that an 'inflation'. There is nothing more deflating than time done on a meat hook.

But on that meat hook, during that terrible time when your children were afraid you would die, I was with you. It was I who brought you back to a life that could include me.

Wait a minute. What do you mean you were with me? I was terribly ill. I was running high fevers. At one point I became conscious of death, looking yellow and pulpy and very unattractive, sitting on my bed. Where were you

---

29 Betty de Shong Meador, *Uncursing the Dark*, p. 31.

then? It wasn't you who helped me get out of that bed to lower my fever with cold compresses and aspirin. It wasn't you who called the doctor. It was me, and the thought of my children. What kind of a good angel are you, to let me almost die? I thought your job was to protect me, to warn me of dangers, to look out for me.

You mortals want to believe that. But I don't operate at that level. That's for your human mother, your human friends and lovers. I don't worry about your sickness or health. I'm just trying to find my way into life through you. I can't tell when I'm too much for you, when I'm a white flash of lightening that can incinerate you. I'm not human, except through you. Life, death, it's all just the turning of the wheel.

No wonder you almost did me in. I saw how dangerous you are. That's when I banished you. It was years later when I read the psychological amplification of the Inanna myth by Sylvia Perera, that I began to understand what had happened to me. She described Erishkigal, Inanna's Sister from Below whose:

> domain, when we are in it, seems unbounded, irrational, primordial, and totally uncaring, even destructive of the individual . . . until the demonic powers of the dark goddess are claimed, there is no strength in the woman to grow from daughter to an adult who can stand against the force of the patriarchy in its inhuman form.[30]

Perera helped me understand that I was in new/old territory, the territory of the goddess, of life as a cyclical process, and that I needed a time of descent "to scoop up more of what (had) been held unconscious by the Self in the underworld," to have more access to my full being, including you, my Erishkigal. When I think of it this way there is no difference, really, between what has gripped me in Jungian psychology and in poetry: myth, the mysteries, the goddess. Maybe what seems to have divided me against myself, torn me in pieces, is all of a piece—one, like the many colors of the peacock's tail in Jung's alchemical amplifications.

I wondered how long it would take you to get to this. I am not your opponent, your enemy, thief of your life energy. I am what animates everything you do and love. I brought you the image of the poet being played like an instrument, the news of the changing myth, of the return of the Goddess. Jung has been a prophet of this shift as well. With the dry Protestantism he grew up with,

---

30 Sylvia Perera, *Descent to the Goddess*, p. 41.

he understood what was missing in Christianity—the feminine. Two thousand years after the death of Virgil, Jung unearthed secrets that have been hidden away in sealed vessels by the alchemists, and are now being brought into consciousness in Jungian psychology, archeology, and in the arts: the old gods are returning, the nature gods, the goddess herself.

It happened so quickly. I remember the days when a woman could not belong to herself and be in a relationship, or so it seemed to many of us. But soon, everything changed. Women were writing poetry. The goddess was in the air. I was in the grip of this change that played me like an instrument, insisted on its music, filled me with the voices of a poetic lineage I was just beginning to realize I was heir to: Enheduanna, Sappho, Mirabai, Goethe, Rilke, Dickinson, H.D., Duncan, di Prima.

And now you seem to be everywhere, not just in me. Poetry is exploding. In a culture that seems fixated on money and celebrity there is a lively other realm in which thousands of poets compete fiercely for publication in small literary magazines for no money and little glory. Why do they do this? Because it is the work of their souls.

In your time, there are many who know me, many who understand that you don't belong just to this life: you have a pact with eternity, a contract with me. Everyone has an essential wild nature that belongs to all time—to the stars, to the trees, to your dreams. It's your aliveness, your spark of the divine. I am a shape-shifter, taking different forms in every one, and many forms in each of you. For some I am your first and only calling. You recognize your "sister or brother from below" from the moment you are born. People recognize this in you. They say: "He has an old soul," or, "She is so totally herself!"

Then there are those who both long for me and fear me, who struggle all their lives to make room for me. Maybe you grew up in a family where I seemed dangerous. Maybe I was a threat to your culture or religion, being fierce and impolite and not concerned about etiquette or ordinary notions of morality. The wild eternal me got stuffed into the cellar with the winter vegetables, or hidden in the closet among your mother's old coats. You became too good, a little hero or martyr, or you disappeared among your peers and became a creature of your time and fashion. I am dangerous from a conventional point of view. My loyalties are not with a particular epoch's prejudices, its fleeting versions of the world. I put my ear to the ground to hear the deepest beat of time: mythic time, millennial time, god's time. If you want respect in your own time don't listen to me too carefully. If all that concerns you is looking good or getting rich forget about what I have to say. But remember, a life lived without me is a life without deep joy, without leaps of imagination, without poetry.

Wait a moment! I'm confused. I thought you were mine. Now it sounds as though you belong to everyone, like you're some sort of world soul.

I am. And I am also yours—your very own particular individual soul. You mortals with your need for definitive shapes. No wonder you have so much trouble understanding that I am one and I am many. Through me you are connected to all time and all beings past, present and future. In their own shape and form, I am contained within all. I am water. You drink me and I join all the juices of your body, I am in your saliva, in your blood. And then you sweat or excrete and I join the flow of waters underground into the sea, I shape-shift into a cloud and rain upon you again.

I am the air you breathe. I enter you and fill you with spirit, and then I'm gone, off to tickle the leaves of a tree, howl in the sky, chase a sail across the water. I am fire. I fill you with intensity, you burn with my sacred language, and then I am gone. I am a guest, a visitor, a passerby. Everyone struggles in some sort of way with me, depressed because I haven't been around recently, or putting me off with a long 'to-do' list, or totally taken over by me, writing poetry all the day long and forgetting to eat.

Longing for Poetry to Arrive

The story that began to reveal itself took you back to your childhood, when I was with you and you were a poet. It was indeed an awful story, about all the blood and slaughter that had preceded you, that blocked you from me, who was your guide before you knew you had one. I'd come to you when you were just a girl. I kept whispering to you even when you weren't listening. You began to reclaim all the poetic little girls in you, but one was missing. You found that wonderful poem of Pablo Neruda's, called "Poetry," about the poetic vocation:

> And it was at that age...Poetry arrived
> in search of me. I don't know, I don't know where
> it came from, from winter or a river.[31]

---

31 Pablo Neruda, *Selected Poems*, p. 457.

The vocation is clear, yet, as you know from your own experience, confused and confusing. Where does it come from? Where does it get its authority? And there you are without a face, naked soul, without persona, and I, the poet within you, touch you. Neruda's poem inspired your own poem, "missing child." You used Neruda's poem as an epigraph. The poem tells the story:

> i have been looking for you
> in all the places the poem
> remembers
> the brick row house in queens
>   dark pond in front
> whiskered cat fish lurking
>   under a lily pad
>   where are you?

> the children of other landscapes
> come to me
> they haven't seen you
> either
> the one who is a horse
> in the ivy woods
> near princeton
> is shaking her mane
> pawing the ground
> racing me across the swinging bridge
> to show me
> her secret
> green cave
> how it turns
> into a magic castle
> a fortress
> a hide out for anne frank—
> the gestapo
> haven't found her
> yet—
> she keeps a diary
> is this where
> poetry arrived?

> or was it
> on that mountain
> path in vermont
> on summer vacation

remember how
crystal lake turned dark
how wild
the currents
of the coming storm
how frantic the trees
the flowers
the winds demanding
words
to say them

or was it
in the piazza del duomo
in florence
a five year old
goes dashing
into a flock of pigeons
shouting
this is where it begins
in this body
this turbulence of wings
this forgotten tongue
this high swoop of church
these doors telling
stories from the bible—

or was it
in the house
on shasta road
not far from where i'm working
on this poem
looking for
the early adolescent girl
i was
through a window pane
in the dark living room
everybody else is out
and she is dancing
to the hot throb of
elvis presley howling
'you ain't nothing but a hound dog'
her parents can't stand
that noise

when the heart beat
drops down
to the groin
poetry
arrives—

the totem pole of all
the children i have been
is falling into place
down to the baby
on a blanket in the sun
tongue reaching for
the shape of sound
before it turns
into a word

except for you—
still lost
somewhere between florence
and the princeton woods

i can't imagine
where you are
until now
half a century later
lying on my face
with acupuncture needles
in the backs of my knees
(which according to traditional chinese medicine
release old blocked energies)—
a door opens—
i see you coming into the house
with your young mother
carrying grocery bags
from the a & p
stomping the snow
off your rubber boots

so small a child
fine hair
delicate features
you can barely breath
the air is thronging with

uninvited

people herded like cattle
people beaten and starved
people forced to take their jewelry off
and walk into gas ovens
people whose frozen toes have been chopped off
                              in the snow

                      for instance your own
father's sister—

no wonder you've been lost
i watch you wandering off
into the 16th century
winter scene by breughel
that hangs over the living room couch
you are standing among the hunters on the hill
returning after a long cold journey
among the dogs sniffing
the scents of earth under the snow
you have no voice
you have no body
you are yearning for the unseen
interior
of some house
tucked away in the valley
in the bottom
corner
near the wooden frame—

              longing for poetry
                                    to arrive[32]

---

32 Lowinsky, *red clay is talking*, pp. 9-13.

Lady of Florence, First Muse

> *Our Lady of the Goldfinch*
> *Our Lady of the Candelabra*
> —H.D.[33]

Who is it I Seek?

The Lady of Florence is in the sound of the church bells. She is in every glimpse of the church of Santa Maria del Fiore, as I turn the dark corner of some narrow street and see her radiance anew. She is clad in white, green and pink marble, in wild contrast to the sombre brown brick of other Florentine monuments such as the Palazzo Vecchio, the old tower of the Bargello, or the Palazzo Pitti. She draws my eyes to Brunelleschi's great red Duomo and suddenly I feel alive, full of inexplicable joy, as though I've come home after a long journey. Do I hear a voice say: "You can never get lost, as long as you keep sight of the Duomo."

The Lady of Florence appears to me like the virgin of the annunciation in the painting by Fra Angelico, surprised out of some deep place, at once disoriented by the news the angel has to tell her, and strangely calm. She glows with gold, like Cimabue's Madonna in Majesty, or in the light of candles, like the Madonna and child tucked into a wall's niche on the street. Someone has made her an offering of fresh flowers. The Lady of Florence is a graceful Italian woman, walking down an old cobbled street in a pair of elegant shoes, or buzzing about on her Vespa, trailing a lovely scarf. There is always some detail that gladdens my eye, fills my heart with something lost yet so familiar. Pope Boniface VIII is said to have remarked that Florentines were the fifth element of the universe. He must be right, for I feel quintissentially myself when I am here. Familiar. Beloved. Yet who is the one who loves me only in Florence? Who is it I seek whom I cannot quite touch?

The Lady of Florence seduces me with gold jewelry and soft leather gloves, enchants me with displays of purple eggplants and red tomatoes nestled in straw in wooden crates outside the little grocery stores. This is the way veg-

---

33 Hilda Doolittle, *Selected Poems*, p. 157. (H.D. refers throughout to Hilda Doolittle.)

etables should look. Suddenly, I am four years old. I want to run into a flock of pigeons in the Piazza Santa Croce and watch them flutter away on their gray-blue wings. Her beautiful language flows all around me. It is so familiar. I expect it to leap from my lips any moment, but it never does. I was a child here. I spoke Italian fluently. Now, in mid-life, I am severed from the tongue I knew when I was four.

Severed, also from whoever it is who loved me so well back then. In the family stories there was a nursemaid, or was she a neighbor, Lydia. I wrap myself in the red and purple shawl I bought at a street fair in Florence, and speak to my inner sister, the one from below. Is this you, I ask her, who makes me feel this way in Florence? Have you always been with me? Did I know you when I was a wisp of a girl?

I was there. I was your first muse. For poetry flourishes in the landscapes of childhood. That is when I first lay my claim, when words are still magic, when trolls lurk under the bridge and trees tell ancient secrets. Everyone is a poet when they are four. That's when I like to shape-shift into somebody impor-tant, usually not of the family, who touches a child's imagination and makes it bloom. I was and was not your Lady of Florence, for she is particular, in a way I am not, to a time and a place you still long for. When you are in Florence you feel that the center of you is in place; it all seems to blossom about you. Yet you know no one, can't speak the language, can't find your way from Santa Maria Novella to San Marco.

Remember, the first time you came as an adult, you dreamt that there was a line of glowing white statues, representing truth, that crossed the Atlantic Ocean from Italy to New York? You had to make your connection to Italy anew, for it was severed when you were five and your family returned to America. You were cut in two then. Your home was not your home. Your language would not return to your lips. The nursemaid, or was she a neighbor, who had loved you and made you feel full of yourself, was nowhere to be found.

But that too, is what it means to be a poet, to be so divided. Look at the Ponte Vecchio, the only bridge over the Arno that survived the Nazi bombings in 1944, with its elegant jewelry shops and its arches. You can see that it is actu-ally two bridges, especially at night. There is the flesh and blood bridge, full of tourists, which you've just walked over, looking at rubies and pearls. There is the other, deeper bridge, insubstantial, with its reflected arches and yellow painted shops in the dark waters of the river. They touch each other, these two bridges, reflect on each other, can't be without each other, and yet are inhabitants, like you and I are, of different realms. Your lost Lydia is like the bridge, dreaming of itself in green waters. It is because of her, that everytime you come to Florence, poetry flows. For it is not just the Lady herself, but the longing for the lady, out of which poetry is made.

Florence of My Father

There are those who would say that Florence is a masculine city, full of towers, Giotto's Campanile, the Bargello, the Palazzo Vecchio, and of course, Brunulleschi's great feat of engineering, my beloved Duomo. In my family story it is the city of my father. It was his work that brought us here, his Guggenheim Fellowship that funded his long hours in the Biblioteca Medici and the Archive of the Duomo, studying the secrets of 16th century Motets in the late 1940s after the end of the second World War. Were he alive he would speak of his admiration for the Florentine Renaissance, how the light of reason and the love of the human body returned to collective consciousness with the revival of classical Roman and Greek knowledge.

My father would tell you stories of the Florentine philosopher Marsilio Ficino, who translated Plato, played the lute, and understood that music was healing to the soul. He would describe the spirit of that time in musical terms, how the Renaissance musician sought a "musical expression free from all shackles,"[34] especially the constraints of a dogmatic church. He would laud the democratic institutions of the Florentine Republic, so far ahead of its time, and point out that the people of Florence gathered in the church of Santa Maria del Fiore not only for religious rituals, but to discuss urban affairs.

My father was a historian of music, a scholar. He believed in critical thinking. There is a cast of mind that has sharp angles, asks hard questions, probes, dissects. That was my father. There is another mode—that of the meander, a glimpse here, an image, a sound, a feeling and suddenly everything brought together as in a rush of wings. I hear a voice say, clear as day: "You'll never be lost as long as you can see the Duomo." My father had no idea his little girl was wandering Florence in the mystical company of the Lady.

What could he know of my Lady? Don't get me wrong. He loved the ladies. He could polish his European charm to a fine glow. He could play the

---

34 Edward Lowinsky, *Music in the Culture of the Renaissance*, p. 28.

energy between himself and a woman like a lute. But did he ever get lost in the Lady? Did she appear to him, then disappear and yet fill him with her radiance? Did he see her everywhere and nowhere? Did he see her in the golden ray entering Mary's ear in the Church of the Annunciation? Did he see her in the sculpted face of Mary in the Pieta by a student of Michelangelo's in the Brancacci Chapel of the Santa Maria del Carmine church? When you look at her from the front, holding her dying son, she looks resigned. But go to the side, look up at her down-turned face and you see unbearable sorrow. For she is the Mater Dolorosa as well as the adoring mother of her child.

Still, if he heard a mass by Palestrina sung in the high vaulted interior of Santa Maria del Fiore, if lovely voices filled that vast space with the sensuality of polyphonic sound, if his heart opened in joy to hear the Ossana, the Benedictus, the Exultate Deo, wouldn't he know the Lady? He must have.

Yet in this play between memory and imagination that brings out the four year old in me, my father has nothing to do with my Lady. He is in the Biblioteca, in the Archive, studying, doing his very important research in the dark. The Lady is out in the light, among the women, my mother, whoever it was who was named Lydia, among the piazzas and churches, the pigeons and cobbled streets, the saints and the stone lions. She is in the eyes of the Madonna which follow me wherever I go. She is in the market, among the women with string bags buying onions and cauliflower. In the Piazza Santa Croce She hovers about the tall African men selling reproductions of Etruscan grave figures. They are as slender and elegant as the twentieth century sculptures by Giocometti. She is in the church itself, where there is a monument for Dante, and where Michelangelo is buried. She is with me as I light a candle for a friend who is dying far away, taking my long white taper and lighting it from a candle lit by someone unknown, someone whose suffering and prayer will remain a mystery as silent as the vast coolness of the Basilica. As everywhere in Florence, there is too much to take in, too many sacred images. I let the Lady guide me: my eyes rise to the agony of the man hanging on the cross, then fall, in the light of many candles, to the baby in the brown-robed arms of St. Anthony.

Dan has done me the favor of falling in love with Florence too. He is the one with the maps. He is the one who knows where we're going. I never know where I am on a map, but I know I am home in my heart. Dan has found us a lovely apartment on the Oltrarno. From the living room window we look out at the river, we can see the Ponte Vecchio, its tumble of shops and windows, its walkers and shoppers. We hear the bells of Florence and the cockamamie song of some bird who produces a prodigious collection of warbles, clicks and gurgles while perched on a clothesline in the inner courtyard. My Lady is in the smell of roasted chicken with rosemary that drifts out of the salumeria across the street from where we live, in the taste of fresh mozzarella cheese, eggplant in olive oil, red wine from Multepulciano. She is in the stone lion fountain at the corner, grinning at me. She is in the flowing skirts that are the new fashion, the big hats, and wide belts. But who was she really, in the flesh and blood of my history. I have called upon my mother for help.

Florence of My Mother

Mother arrives by train from Switzerland. I am blessed in her. She is sturdy, funny, loving, generous. But we are very different in our approach to being women. She has never shared my style, my love of beautiful clothes and jewelry. "Too fancy" she says. As I approach her on the platform, in my purple hat and wide skirt, she exclaims: "How Italian you look!" She couldn't have paid me a better compliment. Has my mother become the Lady? Here, in Florence, in the city of artisans, we shop together like girlfriends; we admire each other in many colored silk scarves; we buy one another amethysts and pearls.

Mother hasn't been here for 50 years. She weeps to see the doors of the Baptistry with Ghiberti's reliefs from the Old Testament. She remembers the stories they tell, of Cain and Abel, of the Flood and Noah's drunkenness, of Solomon and the Queen of Sheba. She remarks on the beauty of the piazzas. She greets Michelangelo's naked David like an old friend. She named my brother after him, the one who was born here. Mother notices an announcement of a concert of Gregorian chant. It is to be in the recruiting center of the military in the Piazza Santo Spirito #9. We walk all over the Piazza looking for #9. I'm ready to give up. She insists on continuing. Unlike me she remembers her Italian. She finds out that the number was wrong but the recruiting center is an arm of the church of Santo Spirito—a lovely Romanesque inner courtyard. Our late 20th century shadows fall on the white wall as the 12th century music rises and falls, it's Gloria, it's Kyrie—the clear voices illuminating the inner courtyard.

I am impressed by how fierce she is about going to the concert, getting there early, holding our seats for us while we paid for dinner. I sit behind her. The amethyst teardrop earrings I bought for her that day catch the light. Her white head leans into the music. At dinner we told her that she was getting more and more beautiful. She is almost 80. Years ago this would have embarassed her. Now she took the compliment, nodded, and said: "I am mostly in harmony with myself. Not always, that would be boring."

We talk about the necessary disharmony that occurs when one goes through changes, when one modulates into a new key. Mother is wise and affirming. The Lady speaks through her. It wasn't always so. My heart was split between the Lady, her radiance, her inwardness—a young woman surprised by an angel—and my hard-working practical mother. "Yes" says Mother, as we walk out of the old part of the city, toward the Campo di Marta, past the train station, the playing field, to the newer section of the city where Mother thinks we lived 50 years ago. "I had the two of you, another on the way. I probably had no time to play with you. There was a nursemaid who helped. Also Lydia. I think she lived downstairs. The only thing I'm sure about is that she had chickens. She was very good with you."

Is Lydia the Lady? Or is it the nursemaid who said: "Mangia, mangia amoretto mio!" That I can remember. I always eat well in Florence. I want my mother to point to a house and say: "This is where we lived. This is where Lydia lived." Nothing comes into such sharp focus. It's all vaguely familiar. The back porch of a house tugs at me. I see a stone lion. I'm sure I know that lion with all my four year old heart. I see, from a distance, the church of seven saints. They stand on high, in front of the church. I know that facade, those saints. But there is no clarity. The lady keeps whispering but I can't quite hear what she is saying.

We are walking on cobblestone streets. Mother is telling the story of my brother's birth. There was something wrong with him. The doctors rushed her baby off before she knew what it was all about. He had a hernia and needed surgery. She slept on straw with the Romany women whose language she did not understand. In the nursery were twins who died. She thought her baby would die too.

We are looking for the hospital. We are tracing her steps. She walked here alone when she was in labor. Where was my father? She walked home alone, leaving her newborn in the hospital, to tend to us, and then back, alone, to nurse him. Back and forth, alone, having just given birth, afraid her baby would die. He lived. My mother walks all over Florence with me, fifty years later. I realize how young she was, in her twenties, younger than all my children are now.

I am always trying to flesh out the Lady. So I keep coming to Florence. Always she talks to me, always she whispers in my ear:

reverie in view of the Ponte Vecchio

lavender chiffon lifts off my shoulders
light wind from the Arno cools
hot flashes

mother in the front room
(came in yesterday by train from Switzerland)
                                    summer rain

such comfort in familiar voices
mother and Dan discussing pregnancies
cousins soon to be born
how beautiful the Jungfrau

mother's voice meanders down
a labyrinth—fifty years since she was last here—
i was a child she pregnant with her third
it was just after the war
the Germans had bombed all bridges except the Ponte Vecchio
(Hitler was fond of it)

mother walked on stones in labor
(long way to the Ospedale Santa Maria di Nuova- Careggi)
slept in the straw with the Romany women
separated from her baby by a sudden flock of white coats—
his emergency surgery—
she remembers

they kept him in a room with sick twins
first they turned green then gray then died
i thought he was next

what is the kernel of this moment?
i want to crack it open eat it
make it a part of my body forever—
> my brother in his brick row house in Toronto
> surrounded by history books—
> the old bridge dreaming of itself
>> in green waters[35]

Lost Story

For a moment, terrible as history is, things make sense. A pattern forms. A poem takes shape. It happens often in Florence. Maybe that's because the city is, as R.W.B. Lewis says, knowable. Such a city, he writes "does good things for one's identity, in knowable surroundings one arrives at a firmer grasp of the self."[36] He contrasts this to how the self gets submerged in the chaos of New York City. Which is where I was headed, when we left Florence. So Florence, divided as it is into quarters, all pulled together by the unifying omphalos of the Duomo, must have organized the four year old me in the way I'm naturally organized. It is a mandala around the center of the Duomo. But around that visible center is all the rich confusion of labyrinthine streets, sudden angles, layers of history, dark corners, famous ghosts.

What happened to the child I was then? In a long ocean liner voyage back to America Mother got sick and Father was helpless when it came to woman's work, like washing diapers. So I did it, stood in for Mother at age five. Then there was New York City, and looking for a place to live, and going to first grade with children who had all been in kindergarten together, feeling like a foreigner, lost between worlds and languages. Nothing made sense. Not until I returned to Florence. Not until the Lady gave me a poem that told me my story.

---

35 Lowinsky, unpublished poem.
36 R.W.B. Lewis, *The City of Florence*, p. 111.

to the lost nurse of a childhood in Florence

1. lost song

in the city where the music began
i hear the song of my life in your voice

yours is the clamorous "te deum" of the bells
yours the fingers of the early morning sun
touching my face and the crown of my head

and when i lift up my eyes
to the window boxes of the via Laura
yours is the gladness of a yellow marigold
the blue arch of the sky
the violet flare of a skirt in the wind and a young woman's laugh
                    on the way to the piazza of the annunciation

            when the two
            who have found one another among strangers
                                embrace

                        where did you go?
                        where is your hand?
                        whose is your voice?

        a cold spread of wings makes sudden the dark of my passage
        there are ghosts that would steal
        the child i once was
                    in your charge
eyes of my skin
ears of my longing
remember me back
to that time

        the war is over in Europe
        weeping pieces of torn apart world
        return to their places
        rebuild their homes

        the great round red head of the Duomo
        is born again in my eyes
        bursting into the sky over Florence

didn't i hear you say
   i would never lose my way
      as long as i kept sight of
         the crowning?

2. lost tongue

in the street there are vegetables
cradled in straw: hot smell of tomatoes
smooth purple eggplants
green bearded cauliflower
mushrooms like gnomes
that have never stopped telling the stories you told
in a tongue i have lost

   a bite of a chicken rubbed with olive oil and rosemary
   tells the tale to my teeth
     of what has been slaughtered
     and what has been cooked
     since i was the one you adored

        you promised so much
        holding the roots of my life in your lap

          before the boat sailed
           to the new world

3. lost god

in the family story
you are the source of my trouble with god
on a morning like this one you carry me deep
into the belly of the church
and a man in dark robes pours waters on my head
and mutters incantations to the god of the strangers
and though my jewish father rages to hear it
        i have been stolen forever—

4. lost story

   what happened to that other story
   of the italian lady you were
   (i wanted to become)

her elegant shoes
> her embroidered wedding sheets
> the man in a hat who was to meet her
> at the train station?

Punch and Judy are fighting in the market
Gepetto carves his cunning son
Grandmama and Red Riding Hood are eaten by the wolf
> again and again
> each time you move the flap
>> under the book

and in the cathedral
where the heart opens to the high vault
> what mystery is it
> that what gathers us together
> must rip us
>> apart?

5. lost ghost

you who are nurse and beloved
wolf and woodcarver
bird that is digested
> in the belly of our loss

be with me now
> and in that perpetual moment
> when the owl calls her mate
>> across the valley

> when the dome of the cathedral
> becomes the belly of the wolf
> becomes the face of the angel
> who knows the whole story

> sing to me
> of the snake that devours its end
> of the great round red head of the sun
> that falls off the ends of the earth
> and is buried by shades of the dead

> there is war again in Europe
> we hide out in the cracked skulls of churches
> our godblasted wings brush the hunger of ghosts

> we who are losers of body and name
> long for the sound of your voice
>
> sing to us
> of the world we once knew in your arms
> of the world we don't know soon to come
> of the dark we are in—
> before crowning[37]

Mother has come and gone and I still don't know who the Lady is. We are such mysteries to ourselves.

Our Lady Reveals Herself

How does one get down to the bottom of oneself, where gold gleams like an old coin, when it is as dark and murky as the bottom of the lake? How do you reach down to the poet you were as a child? I wish I had the access to memory that H.D. does, whose whimsical portrait of her childhood in *The Gift* I so admire. She could be describing my family in this passage:

> No one seemed to belong to Papa when he came in out of the cold, though Mama looked up and Ida said,"Will the Professor want his evening supper now or later?" Everything revolved around him…What it was, was that he was separate, he was not really part of this table with the glass ball, with the tinsel paper, with the workbasket…[38]

H.D. remembers all this. She can trace the imprint of a myth in her poetic young mind from "the dog with his gold-brown wool, his great collar and the barrel…(to) none other than our old friend Ammon-Ra, whose avenue of horned sphinxes runs along the sand from the old landing stage of the Nile barges to the wide portals of the temple at Karnak."[39] I wish I could find the trace of the original lady, the one who was a person, who held and touched me.

My friend Alicia writes from Venezuela. I have sent her a draft of this chapter. She calls the Lady my "first muse." She writes of her own first muse,

---

37 Lowinsky, *red clay is talking*, p. 30.
38 H.D., *The Gift*, p. 43.
39 H.D., *The Gift*, p. 25.

a dark haired American lady who babysat her when she was four, when her Venezuelan family was living in Tennessee. Alicia writes:

> "I remember only the atmosphere of wonder that she represented for me because she connected me with.... another culture and reality, a mystery that even being so little I darkly aspired to. She must have felt something special too, because she gave me a pair of soft black leather gloves, hers. We left the States and the memory faded, but I had these magical super-feminine black leather gloves . . . connecting me with this beautiful woman who represented everything 'Other' that I wanted to be.

Where are my gloves? Where is my something tangible to connect me to the lady? I know her only in landscape. The poet Charles Wright describes my experience:

> Florence is much on my mind, gold leaf and golden frame...
> Mayfire of green in the hills[40]

How can one touch the one who formed you when you can't see her face, can't understand her language? Yet through her come all the other shining sacred ladies: Maria, Sophia, Shakti, the Shekinah, the White Goddess herself. My "Sister from Below" says, rather impatiently, "Use your imagination!"

Oh. Perhaps I should invoke the Lady, the way I did my "Sister from Below." It seems too simple. And yet, when I sit down alone on my poetry porch, wrap myself in my red and purple shawl, and focus inward, she appears. I feel as though I am a child again. Her eyes are green and she looks at me as though I am the world's most beloved child. She is holding me on her lap. My whole body feels alive, sensuous, warm. She is beautiful and in her eyes I feel beautiful. I say, You are here. You remember me.

Of course, because you remember me. I told you I would always be with you. You were so young, I thought you wouldn't understand. But you did. You've come back.

We had a special bond, you and I. I was beyond the age of marriage. The man I was to marry never arrived on that train. He was killed in the war. I never told you that, you were too young. But the life I'd wanted and the child I imagined I would have—a fair-haired little girl who looked like me—were gone. And then there you were, so delicate and small, so burdened with your mother's heavy load. You looked more like me than you did your own mother. People thought you were mine as we wandered the piazzas and you dashed into the

---

40 Charles Wright, *A Short History of the Shadow*, p. 34.

flocks of pigeons, proclaiming your magical powers. Your Italian was so good you could have been mine.

It was a dark period, just after the war. The electricity went off all the time. The heat went off. We sat on our hands to keep them warm. I was always there, in one form or another, feeding you, making much of you. Fresh fruits were hard to come by. I fed you dried bananas. Remember how you loved them?

Your parents were relieved to be back in Europe. America was so strange to them, so uncomfortable. In Italy they felt more at home. So did you. I liked to dress you up. You loved this. I liked to put ribbons in your hair, show you my best dresses, my shoes. I liked to take you out to see the saints, the madonna, to pray in the churches, get you away from the dull neighborhood we lived in, away from my chickens and your mother's washing and cooking.

Sometimes there'd be a puppet show in the piazza: Punch and Judy shrieking at each other, beating each other up. How you loved that. You'd laugh and laugh. You didn't get to be wild in your family. But you were wild with me. I encouraged it. I couldn't bear the thought that you'd be gone from me. But you were not my child. I understood you better than your own parents did. You were so relaxed with me, so playful. Around them you turned into a little grown up. I couldn't bear the fact you had not been baptized, that you'd not go to heaven. Here, in the city of Dante, I wanted you to be baptized so we could be reunited in Paradise. You were all excited about it. You loved the ritual, the Latin prayer, the priest. You told your father. How could you not? You were his child.

He flew into a fury. How could I do such a thing? It was a violation! A desecration! How absurd! I was consecrating you forever. And in any case your father spent more time in churches and knew more about Gregorian Chant and the mass than do most Catholics. I suspected he had a hidden yearning, a secretly Catholic soul. But, as you know, there was no talking to your father. I stayed out of his way.

But something happened to you. You got cut in two. Your father's rage made you afraid of me as you had never been. Yet you longed for me. It broke my heart to see you so divided. Soon thereafter, your family set sail on a big ship to America.

Why don't you come back to me in the flesh? Why don't you let me see you when I'm in Florence? Why didn't you give me a pair of gloves?

What of the shawl you're wrapped in? Don't you remember?

Suddenly I see the eyes of the woman at the street fair in the Piazza della Signoria from years ago, the woman who sold me the red and purple mohair shawl. Looking intently, she handed me the shawl and said, "It will keep you very warm." Was that you? I cry out to the figure of my imagination? Were you always looking for me as I am always looking for you?

Maybe it was me. Maybe it wasn't. Perhaps it's a story you've made up to wrap yourself in when you invoke me, when you write poems. We all make up stories that tell the deeper truths of our lives. Wrap yourself up in my shawl and I will return you to the child you were, the one you lost when you crossed the big ocean and had to wash out diapers in the sink, the one who lost her European footing in America, lost her fifth element, her Firenze. I return you to your poems. Here's one that tells the story in another way.

Lady of Florence, again

the river
your hand on the small of my back
me crossing the old bridge—

> you burst through the gates of my eyes
> light up the back of my skull

> spinal column I rise to greet you
> praising Maria in white marble
> you open the wings of my lungs
> know the way down to my guts

> > your gravity sinks
> > below stones—

i know you in my every breathing cell
but i can't find your face
or a picture of me on your lap as a child

> why don't you run up and greet me
> whirl me around like a girl before time spits me out?

---

it's not about a snapshot a map or the color of my eyes
it's about a bird that sings in the inner courtyard
an old bridge you keep crossing
how seven blue statues of truth are aligned across oceans

in your dream—

> *from Italia to the lady*
> *with a torch in New York harbor . . .*

---

no one knows us in this town we are ghosts visiting
half-lit memories we have a perfectly
adorable make-believe life—
> our apartment requires toilet paper
> milk for tea—

we have taken a train to the city on water gold light winged lions
returned 'home' through a narrow causeway
out of the dream city fancy lady city harlequin city hustler city
to the city of our lady of the white flower—

we are caught in underwater reflections cross currents
the sudden storm that blew the waves backwards

> up river

somewhere in the dark waters is the ghost of a day—

> we are so fleeting to ourselves
> walking down a narrow street
> catching a glimpse of where
> we bought the flowered umbrella
> saw the white figures standing on the hilltop
> > like wordless gods—

---

a lady is giving music lessons in the church
a stone woman is holding the body of her son
we light a candle
we light a candle

i ask you
do you know the river rat
swimming through the arches of the Ponte Vecchio?
do you know the broken old lady her begging bowl
crumbled in the doorway of the church

you tell me
liquid gold is created in the hollow caverns
of your body
face of the dark

Christic is etched into the back

         of your skull—

last night our lady of Florence was in the church Orsanmichelle
tired face of Anne mother of Mary the baby Jesus on her knee

      I am the broken heart of your truth,

                the lost tooth

our lady was wearing a flowing black gown
had a long roman profile dark eyes
played the viola in three of Bach's Brandenberg concertos
or she was the henna haired flirt on the violin
in tight velvet slit above her knee
beckoning her admirers closer

this morning she is wiping clean
the windows with green shutters
of shops on the Ponte Vecchio—

lovely lady none of this comes easily
the streets are full of secret juices humid bodies
vacant men with cardboards signs proclaiming
their hunger—

      we take your photograph
      eat your eggplants soaked in olive oil
      bite into the tart abandon of your artichoke hearts—

in shop windows in blue robes on the sides of churches
skirt slit above the thigh gold frizzled on your head
wearing a hat not wearing a hat
in the Piazza Santissima Annunziata—

        (the muttering priest in the church
        the miracle of how you appeared
        kneeling women lit candles
        golden rays entering your ear—)

our lady reveals herself
in displays of purple radicchio red strawberries
she flows in water under the arches of the old bridge
rides a Vespa her flowered summer dress blows up showing dark thighs
she bargains with me in the clothing store

take me home with you in this soft silk this gauzy gray
stick me in your new leather bag with many compartments—

---

a voice says:

we need to inform you that the garden is closing

> in the Piazza del Duomo
> three tall young Africans
> are selling reproductions—
>   elongated blue Etruscans,
>   (grave figures)
>
>   waving goodbye…[41]

---

41 Lowinsky, *crimes of the dreamer*, p. 48.

How Eurydice Tells It

Hell must open like a red rose

—H.D.[42]

A Visitation

I have been visited by Eurydice. She comes unbidden, unexpected, in the way things usually first come to me—in a poem. But there is something different about how this poem happens. On one of my Fridays devoted to writing, I am suddenly hijacked by Eurydice's point of view, her voice, her demand that I speak for her. She is shrill. She is insistent. She gives me no choice but to work on the poem till I get it how she wants it. She has been much neglected and misunderstood and she lets me know a poem is not enough. It is just the beginning. She wants prose. She wants a chapter in my book. She wants to tell her version of the story.

This haunting by Eurydice is quite astounding—an archetypal shift. I've always seen her as the muse who inspires the male poet, with no female voice, no feminine depths of her own. She is the object of poetic lament, almost raped by the bee-keeping neighbor Aristaeus, killed by snake bite, almost rescued from the underworld by Orpheus who famously, fatally, looks back and loses her forever. She is adored, she is lusted after, she is acted upon, she is victimized, she is longed for, she is sung about, told about, written of in classic literature for thousands of years, but when has she ever been allowed to speak her own truth in her own voice? Now she's telling her story her own way! What an original idea. How very clever of me!

Of course, as Jung has said about complexes—we don't really have ideas; they have us. And, this idea that had me, I soon learn, had previously visited others. One day, as I am leafing through the *American Poetry Review*,[43] a distinguished bimonthly publication in the poetry world, I find an article by one Barry Goldensohn who is a poet and teacher at Skidmore College, tracing Eurydice's dramatic entry into 20th century poetry via Rainer Maria Rilke, the

---

42   H.D., *Selected Poems*, p. 40.
43   *American Poetry Review*, Nov/Dec 1994.

great European poet and contemporary of Jung, and via the great but not as widely known American poet, Hilda Doolittle, who signed her poems H.D.

In Rilke's 1904 poem, "Orpheus. Eurydice. Hermes.," Eurydice is described as being "so loved that from one lyre there came/ more lament than from all lamenting women;/ that a whole world of lament arose . . ." Striking in Rilke's version is that Eurydice has no connection to this world of love and of lament. She is separate from Orpheus, from longing, from life. She is pregnant with her own death. "Deep within herself" says Rilke, "being dead/ filled her beyond fulfillment."[44] For the first time we see Eurydice as disengaged from Orpheus' plan for her. She has her own reality. She belongs to herself and to death.

Just twelve years later we hear her voice in the fierce tongue of H.D., addressing Orpheus directly. Now, Eurydice is in a fury:

> so for your arrogance
> and your ruthlessness
> I am swept back
> where dead lichens drip
> dead cinders upon moss of ash
>
> so for your arrogance
> I am broken at last,
> I who had lived unconscious,
> who was almost forgot;[45]

In a remarkable shift, for the first time since the beginning of the myth, Eurydice is in a rage. She has been disturbed, awakened, only to be sent back to the underworld. And it is <u>her</u> lament that fills the poem, lament for the world she has lost yet again:

> all, all the flowers are lost;
>
> everything is lost,
> everything is crossed with black,
> black upon black
> and worse than black...[46]

---

44 Rilke, *Selected Poems*, p. 51.
45 H.D., *Selected Poems*, p. 36.
46 H.D., *Selected Poems*, p. 37.

To my chagrin, I realize that my brilliant idea had visited Rilke, H.D. and Goldensohn among others, long before coming to me. This is deflating. But worse yet, I realize while reading Goldensohn's article, that I know Rilke's poem, have read H.D.'s poem, have admired both—but failed to understand what the poems say about the changing myth—until Eurydice made her presence known directly to me. It seems I don't really get ideas until they really get me. And the way this happens is through poems. Poems get me by taking me over, filling me with images, wrestling with me for days and waking me up in the night until they get their essential selves through to me, teach me the words to say them. When Eurydice grabbed hold of me, she began to teach me her changing nature.

I must apologize, at this point, for the hubris of including my own poem in the same context as the poems of two of the greatest 20th century poets. Rilke gives me an out. The Sister has already reminded us of that famous quote in which Rilke says: "Ultimately there is only *one* poet, that infinite one who makes himself felt, here and there through the ages, in a mind that can surrender to him"[47](and we should add, *her*). I imagine that poet to be the deep changing myth, the ever-changing mind of the gods, the ongoing creative work Jung describes as visionary. It was only after Eurydice came to me that I could see what she was doing in Rilke's poem, and in H.D.'s.

My Father's Myth

Learning to listen to the mythic level, to hear the poetry of the changing myth, is like that moment when you suddenly hear the birds singing. You can go around in your life and hear the telephone and your spouse and the traffic noises and then suddenly one day notice that the birds *are singing*. They've been singing all along but suddenly you hear them—and now you begin to hear them all the time. Poetry is like that. Suddenly you hear it, and realize its around you all the time. Like bird song, its something you used to hear, when you were a child, and have forgotten, and must remember.

Poetry came to me early. I can remember the moment. I was nine. I was in Northern Vermont, where my family went for the summers. I was walking down a mountainside. I see myself alone. Could I have been? Or were my

---

47 Gass, *Reading Rilke,* p. 183.

parents and brothers on the trail behind me? A storm was brewing. Clouds were turning deep blue gray. The air shifted, energy rising in the atmosphere and suddenly I had the experience that the trees, the wind, the waves on the lake were all speaking to me. They were filling me with energy and feeling. Words began coming—a rhythm—an intensity of colors. I was the human voice of the pine trees, of the lake waters, of the darkening sky. They were all gathering to be said by the poem moving through me. Then I understood that one way to be a poet was to be the human mouth of the natural world.

The myth of Orpheus and Eurydice came to me early as well. I cannot remember a time I did not know them. They were as much a part of my imaginal world as were Hansel and Gretel, Abraham and Isaac, Pinnochio and Geppetto. I owe this to my father. He was a professor in the music department at the University of Chicago for twenty-five years. My father was a shape-shifter. He could be intensely focused inward, hearing a musical phrase, or working out some problem of scholarship in his mind, not hearing a thing you said. He could be intensely focused outward, arguing about politics and history and events on the world stage. He could fly into rages, mostly in German, sometimes in Dutch or Italian or English. And, in my favorite mode, he could be spellbinding, a charmer of the form of wildlife called young children, a teller of marvelous stories, a fabulous musician—in short, the embodiment of Orpheus himself! Fitting, since my father's period of expertise was the Renaissance, during which Orpheus shape-shifted rapidly after more than a thousand years of being Christianized, and regained his Greek magic.

In reading for this chapter, suddenly I find myself among Father's old cronies. Footnotes, references are to the men who came over for dinner in my childhood, Renaissance scholars whose names connoted mysterious adult dramas to my young ears. I hear my father's impassioned voice in the midst of some iconographic or theological dispute yelling in person or in out-loud fantasy at Panofsky, Kristeller, or Nino Pirrotta.

But there was no conflict when it came to Orpheus. The Orpheus of my childhood was filled with a golden light. His lyre was magical.

The Orpheus of my childhood was that Renaissance version of Orpheus who could charm the wildest animals, the most unruly children, settle them down, get them to sleep. He even charmed the scary black dog that guards the gates of hell, and the ghosts and goblins on the way down into the underworld relaxed when Orpheus played, they let him down where no one alive had gone before, and even the terrible King and Queen of the Underworld were charmed by his music, lulled into a sweet reverie, and gave him leave to bring his Eurydice back up. Only don't, said the Queen, under any circumstance, look back, or you'll lose her.

Identifying with Orpheus, how could one not look back? One would keep straining to hear her footsteps; one would not be sure if one could hear them; one would have to look back.

The Orpheus of my childhood was that Renaissance version which envisions him as musician, poet, civilizer. I had not yet encountered the primitive Orpheus, the priest of Dionysus, the shaman, or heard the story of his being rent to pieces by the Maenads. In recent years, with the help of many conversations with Joseph Henderson and a fine paper called "Orpheus, the Lyre Player"[48] by Gary Astrachan, I've come to see Orpheus as a bridging figure between pagan and Christian worlds, and between Eastern and Western religious attitudes. Joseph Henderson describes Orpheus as the "god who remembers Dionysus, but looks forward to Christ."[49] In some versions of the myth Orpheus is a priest of Dionysus who reforms that wild religion, bringing an eastern inwardness to the ecstatic experience. He is, in Astrachan's words: "a radical reformer of Dionysiac religion, leading his followers from meat, flesh-eating and the hunt, to a spiritual communal vegetarianism."[50]

But none of that was part of my father's myth. Nor did Eurydice make more than a cameo appearance in my father's version. The Eurydice of my childhood was a pale, wan *shikse*[51] disappearing into darkness, a bloodless Mary dressed in blue, being visited by a sexless angel, a Botticelli Venus so blond and blue eyed, so slim and perfect no woman has ever been her. I did not find her very interesting, not until she called upon me.

---

48 Gary Astrachan, "Orpheus, the Lyre Player," *Harvest*, 1992.
49 Joseph Henderson, *Man and His Symbols*, p. 145.
50 Astrachan, "Orpheus, the Lyre Player," *Harvest*, 1992 p. 104.
51 A 'shikse' is a non-Jewish young woman. The kind a Jewish mother wouldn't want her son to marry.

The Voice of Rot

When sitting down to work on this chapter, I knew I needed more than the poems—Rilke's, H.D.'s, my own. I needed an ongoing conversation with Eurydice. So I invoked her in active imagination and was startled at how quickly she appeared, as though she were the thirteenth fairy, just waiting to be invited. I can see her now, trailing grave clothes, like Rilke's Eurydice. A dark veil covers her face. She carries a red hibiscus flower, with its cluster of yellow pollen on a long sexual stalk. She keeps changing her form. She is a ghostly wraith, a dark specter, a shifting cloud. Sometimes her dark eyes are aglow behind her mysterious veil. Sometimes they are black eye sockets and the veil has turned into black mummy, strips binding her head. She goes from evocative to ghastly, from mysterious to ghostly, from enticing to terrifying. And she speaks:

You have kept me away too long. I've been waiting for thousands of years. I'm not interested in all this stuff about your childhood and your golden Orpheus. You said you'd let me do the telling!

Oops. I guess she's mad at me. Eurydice, I will let you do the telling. But I had to set the stage. I can't just let you come out like that without any preparation. You're scary!

Come now, your readers appreciate the underworld. Why else would they pick up a book called "The Sister from Below?" You've kept them waiting 'til the fourth chapter to even hear from me, who really speaks for the underworld.

Okay. I'll get out of your way. It's all yours!

I am not that pretty one you think I am, or only briefly, for fleeting moments. I am the black hole, the void, the dead place you fear when you are suffering. I am the part that gets left out, has been since Sumer, since Inanna went down to the underworld, the place of rot, the putrefying flesh, Inanna on her meat hook.

I am the black earth of the soil being turned—

the worms are of me

the maggots are of me

Orpheus wants to keep me young and beautiful. He denies my ancient nature. He forgets I am nature.

I am the woman in the ancient menstrual ritual, the Thesmophoria; after they have slit the throats of the baby pigs, and fed them to Snake who lives in the pit, the chasm, the cave, the void—I am the one who brings the rotten meat back up from the dark place to feed the fields.

Am I disgusting to you? Look into these black holes, my eyes—see how swiftly I turn beautiful—a veiled priestess—guardian of the mysteries. I am both. I am much more. I am here to remind you of the part of the cycle you want to forget—to deny. I am the voice of rot, of what falls apart and is eaten by vultures, hyenas. The whole thrust of your culture, your last three thousand years, has been to leave me behind. Orpheus wants to bring me back up, transform me, transcend me. Anything but embrace the whole of me.

All of your roots dig down into me, and all your life routes will take you to me one day—

that you will die is food for your soul—

that there are dead is food for your soul—

Everything grows out of me—blooms, dies back into me. I am the dark part of the creative, the mold of change, the ferment of transformation that makes wine out of grapes, bread out of wheat, beer out of hops. Nothing can change without my dark intervention. I am the light of the dark, the turn of the earth at the bottom of the cycle, the moment after the exhalation, when breath returns to the body.

When Kore went down into the underworld her mother made a deal—got her back for part of the year—but did not deny Kore her time down under. That is why the mother daughter mystery, though men don't take it very seriously, honors a woman's wholeness. Daughters become mothers and have daughters who become mothers. They get their time down there in the underworld.

Before Plato, before Aristophanes, in poems that are lost, there was a time when Orpheus was successful in bringing me back. He was still close to the ancient roots of the religion that knew women. In those days we were equals, lovers in the full sense. That was a very long time ago.

More recently he has lost his feeling for the underworld. Though a priest of Dionysus, the god who knows women, he has no real interest in women. He prefers his big lament. He loves lamenting me. This gives him an excuse to pay no attention to women. He canonizes me. I am the pure white fig leaf of his imagination, his lost but forever shining soul—he can forever be in love with his Eurydice—but not have to muck around with real women or with what goes on "down there." He can be pure. I can be pure in his imagination. He has no idea of what has been being brewed down in that witches cauldron of the underworld over three thousand years of women being split off from our deepest nature.

I used to be a great queen, a fierce goddess. My name means "wide ruler." I have also been called Agriope—Savage Watcher, Queen of the Night, Persephone, all those stories about Helen are really stories about me.[52]

But Orpheus wants to worship the sun and forget about the night. He left me behind in the Bronze Age—left me with the ancient clay goddesses you living are only now beginning to rediscover—those goddesses with big hips, intricate designs carved into them, with heads of snakes or birds eyes and beaks for nipples. He left me in the dark, while he went on to become many versions of himself: shaman, singer, poet, priest. My only life has been in his imagination.

He crossed over the threshold. He says he wants me back—that he would do anything to get me back. But note—the me he wants back is a purified Eurydice, a refined Eurydice—a pretty Eurydice—without snakes, dark origins, rot, rage and sex. Plato has him preferring rebirth as a swan to birth from the body of a woman. He does not want to originate from my darkness.

Now, tell me truly, who is it who has been dismembered? Whose head has been severed from the rest of her body?

Can you see why I rage at Orpheus? He has left so much out—all the blood and the lust, the confusions, the detumescence of the many moons, the falling apart time—the premenstrual engorgement, the bitching, the sharp teeth, the bull that gets torn apart and eaten raw—he wants to rise above all this and leave the great female cave in the dark, leave the Dionysian orgy of—which I am Queen—

death is an orgy of sex—

the underworld is full of the union of differing natures

carnivorous coniunctionis

we all become one—we all eat each other are eaten by each other come in and out of one another become each other become one another's bodies become our mother earth.

---

52 John Warden, Editor. *Orpheus: The Metamorphosis of a Myth*, p. 16.

Orpheus wants to rise above all this. He wants to come rescue me—his pure one—his bride. He wants to sever me from myself, cut me off from my whole nature.

It's an impossible situation. If I respond to him, he denies the greater part of me. If I ignore him, I lose the part that dances on earth with him. This has been going on for a long time—this dismemberment of who I am. Isis is always trying to put Osiris back together. But when have you seen Orpheus trying to put me back together? What is the matter with these men? They dismember us and then prefer us that way! "Let's take this breast—part object I think you call it in your field—this lovely face with long blond hair—and leave the smelly rest down there where it belongs."

I have been working my way back into my own myth for millennia. I had to start with men who were open to me, because so few women since Sappho have had access to the pen. There was a glimpse of light in Virgil. He only gave me a couple of lines in his 4th Georgic, but what I liked in his version was not the telling of my story, but how he told the story of Aristaeus, the beekeeper whose attempt to rape me is the beginning of my initiation into the mysteries. I ran away and was bitten by a snake. You know the rest.

In Virgil's version, Aristaeus' bees have all died because he was the inadvertent cause of my death. Now that makes sense to me. Bees are the sexual energy of the world of plants and flowers. Without them nothing can breed. Virgil is describing an ecological disaster that is the result of an affront to me. It's like Demeter stopping the grain from growing. What must be done to set the world right again? A sacrifice. And what must be sacrificed? Four bulls and four cows—on the altar of the nymphs. The bulls of Dionysus, the cows of Hathor. Killed and left to rot. And after eight days a swarm of bees rise from their bodies.

Life comes out of death, out of the rot. Virgil understands what it is that needs to be honored, in order to bring the world back into harmony.

But it's a long time before anyone else gives me a voice, shows any understanding or appreciation of who I am. It's all about Orpheus—who once he has lost his pretty idea of me begins to reject women. Ovid has him turn to boys. Clement of Alexandria turns him into a celibate singing the new song of Christ, forgetting the old song I sing, from a time before history, before writing.

When the Christians got me they de-sexed me, turned me into a she-eunuch to protect their pure spirit. Or they turned me into a she-devil. Boethius came right out with it. For him I represent those disgusting earth bound passions that keep Orpheus from God.[53] *In the Renaissance they tried to turn me into Wisdom. I suppose I should be flattered. But it's just all so disembodied, so sexless. I can't find my whole nature anywhere. It took until Goethe in the early 19ᵗʰ century for my Helen nature to be given a voice, to be freed from the eternal realm of the Mothers, and let out to play with Faust for a short while. But not for long.*

And then at long last, that poem of Rilke's that you mentioned at the beginning. Finally I belong to myself. Finally I belong to my death. Finally the weight of the poem is with me. I am female, pregnant with all the heavy weight of what for so long has not been born of me. I am absorbed in my own mystery. I am root. Orpheus is impatient, he's immature. He laments me. He's not really with me—he is in his own world, his lament world. Hermes is the one who walks with me. Listen to how Rilke understands me:

> But now she walked beside the graceful god,
> her steps constricted by the trailing graveclothes,
> uncertain, gentle, and without impatience.
> She was deep within herself, like a woman heavy
> with child, and did not see the man in front
> or the path ascending steeply into life.
> Deep within herself. Being dead
> filled her beyond fulfillment . . .
>
> She was already loosened like long hair,
> poured out like fallen rain,
> shared like a limitless supply.
>
> She was already root.[54]

Rilke knows me as death maiden, as flower root, as falling rain. But he does not know my rage, or my rot.

And what of Jung? He is of the same generation as Rilke. Do you see him as understanding your rage and your rot? Did he contribute to your coming back to life? It seems to me his nature was Orphic, not so much in the poetic sense, but in the priestly and prophetic sense.

Jung learned everything he knew from the women I haunted, beginning with that fifteen year old girl, his cousin, who was a medium. Visionary women get their wild raw stuff from me. Jung, to his credit, listened to them, and within the

---

53 Orpheus, *The Metamorphosis of a Myth*, p. 68.
54 Rilke, *Selected Poems*, pp. 51, 53.

limits of his gender and culture, honored me in them. He had a feeling for the
mysteries I serve. I like it when he says:

> Emptiness is a great feminine secret. It is something absolutely alien to man;
> the chasm, the unplumbed depths, the yin . . . A man may say what he likes
> about it; be for it or against it, or both at once; in the end he falls, absurdly
> happy, into this pit, or, if he doesn't, he has missed and bungled his only
> chance of making a man of himself.[55]

And he opened the eyes and the hearts of the women around him to me. All
those Jungian women writing about the Orphic frescoes at the Villa of Myster-
ies in Pompeii, where for a brief moment, two thousand years ago, before the
volcano exploded, women were initiated into my mysteries. They understood
an aspect of my path: a woman has to go "through the lower way" in order to
become herself.

But what woman has given me voice, in the two plus millennia since Enhed-
uanna wrote, since Sappho loved, since the Shulamith sang her **Song of Songs***,*
since language has been taken over by men because they knew how to read it
and write it and kept women out of the priestly caste, the literate caste. Orpheus
likes to claim to be unworldly. But from the beginning, from the first poetic frag-
ment, he has been known as "famous Orpheus." He was seen as one of the origi-
nal trinity of poets with Hesiod and Homer while I've been forgotten. Orpheus
got famous and left me behind in the dust. Orpheus went off with Jason and the
Argonauts through the dangerous narrow passage, to find the Golden Fleece—
forgetting that I am the narrow passage, the dangerous birth canal through
which all human life must pass.

Who spoke for my rage and my loss until H.D. did, in this century? Who
knew how angry I am at Orpheus, how I understand his projection on me. How
I lament the loss of the flowers. How my hell is no worse than his. How even in
the dark I have more fervor than he. How even in hell I have my own thoughts,
my own spirit, my own self. Listen to her rant:

> what was it that crossed my face
> with the light from yours
> and your glance?
> what was it you saw in my face?
> the light of your own face,
> the fire of your own presence? . . .

---

55 *The Archetypes and the Collective Unconscious*, CW, Vol. 9i, par. 183.

all, all the flowers are lost;

everything is lost,
everything is crossed with black,
black upon black,
and worse than black
this colorless light...

my hell is no worse than yours
though you pass among the flowers and speak
with the spirits above earth . . .

hell must open like a red rose
for the dead to pass.[56]

So the dead have passed through and I've come back to life, to myth, to poetry, through H.D. who remembers me. She returns my head to my body, my voice to my passion, my sex to the daylight, my erotic dreaming, my hot language, my rot, my rage.

When the Dead don't get their Due

For years now I have been working on you, preparing you to receive me. We hung out, though you didn't exactly know it. Remember all those years you were so haunted by your dead? You had to climb your way out of all that rot to find your own voice. There were great disturbances among those dead. They couldn't settle down. They couldn't come to terms with their deaths. Dead without proper burial, without help from the living in their passage to the other world, are a dangerous crew. They can't sink into their own fates, die down into their slow changes, become dust of dust, ashes of ashes, join the ferment of everything becoming everything else.

When the dead don't get their due, when they are not properly buried or burned or scattered or mourned or accompanied into the next world by prayers from the living, they create a serious disturbance in the balance of things. The underground can't swallow them. They get regurgitated into the realm of the living, in nightmares, in hauntings; the living don't know what's getting under

---

56 H.D., *Selected Poems* pp. 37, 39-40.

*their skins, into their restless unfocused thoughts, into their lives that feel crazy
and ungrounded.*

You mean the properly buried dead don't haunt the living?

*Sure they do. Your father has clearly been haunting you, demanding to be
remembered as more than a negative father complex, sticking books in your
face—Goethe's Faust, Rilke's Elegies, essays on Orpheus. He has haunted you
into this writing so you could understand who Orpheus was in him, and in you.
But this is all part of a natural process—the work of the living is to digest the
dead. The work of the dead is to be digested, by the earth, by the world of plants,
animals, waters, the unconscious. But mass graves, who can digest that? Ethnic
cleansing? Thousands burnt to death in falling towers, who can digest that?
You've learned with my help, though you haven't known it was me, to write
poems in the voices of the dead. It's the only way to digest the indigestable. You
wrote a poem like that about September 11th.*

voices from the ashes

where is my body?
who brushed teeth kissed the baby made the early train?
whose spirit's been knocked beyond breath?
whose soul keeps running down a gone stairwell?

who brushed teeth kissed the baby made the early train?
whose burning heart whose exploding lungs?
whose soul keeps running down the gone stairwell?
where are my bones?

whose burning heart whose exploding lungs?
who wanders streets shows strangers your smiling blown up photograph?
where are your bones?
take my blood it's all i have to give

who wanders streets shows strangers your smiling blown up photograph?
whose hole whose holy whose ground zero?
take my blood it's all i have to give
watch my red life stream into vials and vials

whose hole whose holy whose ground zero?
i give you the life you stunted bombed in Baghdad made a prisoner of Sharon

watch my red life stream into vials and vials
for i with only a box knife have brought your towers down

i give you the life you stunted bombed in Baghdad made a prisoner of Sharon
i have crashed your Pentagon i am David i am Geburah
for i with only a box knife have brought your towers down
i am your nightmare i poison your waters i blow up your bridges

i have crashed your Pentagon i am David i am Geburah
you the high and mighty carry buckets sift through rubble
i am your nightmare i poison your waters i blow up your bridges
steel has melted buildings keep burning all is sulphur

you the high and mighty carry buckets sift through rubble
we come from the same story your Abraham is my Ibrahim
steel has melted buildings keep burning all is sulphur
your ashes are my ashes

we come from the same story your Abraham is my Ibrahim
the veil is ripped Azazel the wicked has his day
your ashes are my ashes
where is the angel Raphael healer of war wounds guide in hell?

the veil is ripped Azazel the wicked has his day
where is your body?
where is the angel Raphael healer of war wounds guide in hell?
whose spirit's been knocked beyond breath?[57]

You couldn't tolerate the times you live in without my help, without what you learn from the voices of the dead. Without us there is no life. We are the beginning and we are the end. I bring you my nasty side, my Maenad nature, my Thracian origins. I speak for the sharp tongues of women. We too are poets. We have our own way of worshiping the gods. We are daughters of a mystery we are beginning to remember. Remember me in my fullness. Remember me for who you were and will be again. Remember us both with your poem.

I still feel funny putting my Eurydice poem in the same context as the work of Rilke and H.D.

Oh, come off it! You didn't really understand Rilke and H.D.'s poems before you wrote your own. You needed me to visit you before you could understand how I visited them. I come to many poets in many different ways. But you are

---

57 Lowinsky, *Psychological Perspectives*, 2002.

*the **only** you. I am one of the many forms your "Sister" takes. Without me there would be no book, no poetry. So end my chapter as you began it—with the poem I gave you:*

How Eurydice Tells It

When the slashed sun bleeds
                    the end of the day
And the banshee moon arouses
                    the dark one

                    I am transported
                    out of my married bed
                    to the place where time
                                        cracks open—

                    Snake bites
                    a river is crossed
                    flesh falls
                    my heart is offered up

                    to the lust
                    of the ancestors
                    and the old queen rattles
                    the bowl of my bones
                    she teaches
                                        the rutting
                                        of rot

But Orpheus
lost husband
sees none of this
he has come to make a music
to spirit me back
                    to the sky—
                    so pure his song
                    so luminous
                    his eyes—

the very shades cease
                    their hullabaloo
                    and animals dream

of the light
He beckons
until the sun dances
on the leaves and he has turned
his backlit face
                to see me
                        unveiled—

My story is different
than the one men tell:
        For whom he sees is not
                his sweet Eurydice—
                a young wife
                        terrified
                        of snakes

        My eyes are basilisk
        My hair is maenad
                and I am doing
                the dirty dance
                the queen of bones taught me
                                down there

Song sticks
  in his throat
        hand rises up
        to cast me back
                        into the black

                        forgetting I have always been
                                a Thracian woman
                                me and my sisters—

                        Bull dances in our hips
                        Bull bleeds the spent moon
                        ours is the rhythm
                        ours is the music
                        ours is the mystery
                                        that cracks time
                        cracks Orpheus

When the banshee moon arouses
                    the dark one
                    a living sun
                    is sacrificed
                    each day

                    give us this night
                    our harrowed flesh
                    the old gods' spell is rising through
                    the roots of the rose

And you who still mourn
                    Orpheus

I ask you
had he never
looked back
had he never
to save his
                    idea of me
                                        flung me away—

would you take my hand
in the flowering world
would you hear me out
of the spell of the dead
would you bow to my rising
would you dance to my song
would you look into
                    my basilisk eyes?[58]

---

58 Lowinsky, *red clay is talking*, p. 90.

A Grandmother Speaks from the Other Side

Forgive me my sisters
I have taken your silence into my heart
There it lives and suffers…
                    —Nelly Sachs[59]

Is there a Muse in the House?

Stuck. What comes next? What wants to be written? I'm sitting here on my poetry porch on a day with time to write and nothing to say. Is there a muse in the house?

Blank page. White Very white. Write about the white page . . .

Sister, my Sister from Below whose big idea this whole project is . . . where are you when I need you?

I'm right here.

Then why aren't you saying anything? Why are you so still?

I'm listening.

But I've got nothing to say. That's my problem.

Not to you. I'm listening to who is blocking you. When you're blocked it's usually because there is a voice that you don't want to hear.

Who would that be?

Quiet. I'm trying to hear. She says she's your grandmother. Her name is Clara.

---

59 Nelly Sachs, *O the Chimneys*, p. 257.

Clara! She's the grandmother who died before I was born. What can she want from me? I haven't neglected her. Actually, I've spent a great deal of time with her in my imagination!

You sound upset.

I am. Not about Clara. I am glad I got to know her in the way one gets to know a ghost. It's about the Shoah, the terror my people come from. I have written a lot about it, paid my dues so I thought. I don't want to go back there.

Well, you have offended your grandmother. She says you wrote a whole chapter about the dead, and never once mentioned her. She thought you and she had an agreement, that you would remember her.

We did have that agreement. And I've never forgotten her. I wrote about my Jewish dead. What does she want from me? This is a book about writing, about the muse. I don't think she fits in here.

She clearly disagrees. I'm getting out of the middle of this. This is between you and her!

Her Mark on Me

My ghost grandmother, who visits me in phrases, in bits of story, in glimmers across large bodies of water, is speaking to me again.

You will never be done with the Shoah. It will always be a part of you. You will just come at it from different angles at different times of your life. The Shoah took me from you, it took your grandfather, it forced your mother's parents to leave Europe with their daughters and their son-in-law, my son. You have promised to remember me, and to live fully the years that were stolen from me. How can you speak of the dead and never mention me by name? How can you write about the muse and not remember me? Haven't I inspired you? Given you many poems? Don't you know that ancestors are muses too?

How about your other grandmother, whom you call Oma, isn't she a muse to you? Hasn't she just revisited you and didn't you respond with a series of poems? In one poem you actually invoke her. So why am I forgotten? And didn't you meet the ghost of your grandfather Leopold, my wayward husband, when you were recently in Holland, and didn't he speak to you? It seems to me we ances-

tors have been very generous with you. You need to return the favor. To write out of what haunts you is to ground yourself in where you come from, and to pay respect to those whose only expression is in your words.

But grandmother, I can't do that without going back into the territory of the Shoah. I thought you understood that it's bad for me to focus on that terror. It can become a habit, a paralysis. In the stories I've heard, you are always sensitive to children's needs, to their developmental issues. I'd imagine you would understand the issues of my childhood, when terror was my familiar, how it lived in the beleaguered air of a household filled with ghosts: the six million, you, my grandfather, Anne Frank. Your deaths were intertwined in my young psyche with Anne Frank's story, and with the guilt that I lived and she didn't. Terror petrified me, made it hard to be a child, to play, to lay my claim on life.

Terror came roaring down the stairs shouting in my father's voice. His fury was soul murdering. He enacted Hitler. Terror came on the news at six. We listened as we ate dinner. It was 1952, in Princeton, New Jersey. My father was the first humanist to be invited to the Institute for Advanced Studies. His colleagues were the famous physicists Oppenheimer and Einstein, himself a refugee from the Shoah. On the newscast we heard the terrifying voice of Joe McCarthy. The House UnAmerican Activities Committee, was about to go after Oppenheimer and Einstein. To my young mind the committee was the same as the pogroms against the Jews you and grandfather had fled in Russia, the Nazis you'd tried to flee, that my parents and my mother's parents fled. I thought you understood that I was stalked by terror, as by a big cat. I was the prey animal. How could I be wild, free, experimental with my life? I lived in a narrow world, hoping the beast wouldn't notice me. Perhaps, if I didn't really inhabit my life, I wouldn't be snatched out of it. I learned slowly, picking my way through dreams filled with Nazis and Cossacks, that in order to grasp my own individual life, to have my own days and nights, suns and moon, to find my own path, I had to shake off the terrors of the six million, of Anne Frank, your terrible story. I had to live in my own time and in my own culture.

You are no longer a child. You have made a full life for yourself. It is time you face what haunts you.

But grandmother, I have. I wrote about my family history of the Shoah in *The Motherline*[60] and in many poems in *red clay is talking*.[61] I knew I needed

---

60 Lowinsky, *The Motherline.*
61 Lowinsky, *red clay is talking.*

to follow the ancestral connections of my motherline through what the Germans call *Die Schreckenjahre,* the "Terror Years." In writing *The Motherline* I came to realize the obvious: I was the first grandchild born in the New World, after all the deaths and dislocations. No wonder I was so burdened, so marked, so tied to the only grandparent I knew, my mother's mother, my Oma. In the writing of *The Motherline* you, who died in a concentration camp before I was born, began speaking to me, and I saw how profoundly I was haunted. In Anne Michaels' novel about survivors of the Shoah, *Fugitive Pieces,* she described how it was for me:

> my ear was pressed against the thin wall between the living and the dead…
> the vibrating membrane between them was so fragile.[62]

Through that fragile membrane, you visited my life. And now here you are again. I gave you a whole chapter in *The Motherline.* But you are not satisfied. You say it is not enough. You came to me in a poem in which I recognized how you had been with me since childhood. It is written in your voice. Here it is, in case you don't remember it.

a grandmother speaks from the other side

again, the pyramid of skulls
H.D.

don't leave me out
you don't know how often
i've touched you
since i first felt you leap
fish out of the blue
in the new world

i took cancer's way out
of the barbed wire
concentration camp
pulling your right eye
to wander after me
before you were even born
that was my mark
in passing

---

62   Anne Michaels, *Fugitive Pieces,* p. 31

some call it a lazy eye
we know it's the eye that sees
the other world

your parents
made every attempt
to correct
your vision

black patch on a baby face
grey metal optical machine
that hurt the bridge
of your nose when you were six

the lady with beehive hair
told you to make the boy
you saw with your left eye
play with the baseball
you saw with your right eye

your head hurt
you couldn't make it happen
no one in your family
played ball they played
the violin
the piano
the symphonic station
on the radio

your father
my son
kept a photograph of me
on a textured yellow shawl
with black fringe
on the grand piano

the lid of my left eye droops
eye of grief and prophesy
even now
the future i was seeing
cannot be
imagined

it took two operations
the ether mask
coming down on you
the last number you heard
was 99
it was i who turned you back

it's not your time i told you
like i did
when my daughter out of auschwitz

came to live in your room
put a spell on
         you

almost left
your body
your mother was sick in bed
your father listening to
Schubert's unfinished symphony

behind closed doors
no one could disturb him
it was i who banged
on his heart to make him see
                  you wandering off

            in the direction of your right
                      eye—
           in the meadow of the shadow
                  a rock

           a coiled green and yellow snake
           an open mouth
           you almost falling in
                  to my realm—

your father's urgent hands
that flung you over his shoulder
the needle in your arm
the hospital room
when they took the bandages off your eyes

the world had gone
crooked—

stairs at weird angles
walls and corners
on the radio
the army mccarthy hearings
some of the hounded voices are people
your father knows
it is your job to keep your eyes on
the ones who are after us
they took me away
they're coming back
every day in bed recovering
from surgery
you prepare a complete report
they put oppenheimer on the stand
they're accusing einstein
their voices growl and bark
point of order mr. chairman
point of order!

i fade
your eyes
hitched together
have stopped seeing
things

you have turned
the age i was when everything

                                    stopped—

the train to auschwitz that took
your grandfather
the pyramid of skulls
that is
my grave

don't leave me out
i've let you be for many years
this is the time of life i never got to live
you need my eye
of grief i need your wandering eye

—that sees
me—

i'm here
i've made my mark
on you[63]

History is the Poisoned Well

How can you say I'm ignoring you? That poem was my covenant with you. You were the one who helped me understand that it did not serve you for me to live in a state of terror, of paralysis. What good is it for me to lose my life as well? You encouraged me to build a firewall between me and the Shoah, to put terror away, not dwell with horror. I lived a personal life, enjoying the blessings of America. But after September 11ᵗʰ I found myself in the grip of a strange feeling—one that felt blasphemous to say aloud. I felt relieved. By what? Suddenly everyone around me inhabited a world I knew so well, a world I shared with you, my ghostly grandmother, with my family, with my people, a world where the terrible can happen at any moment. During my period of feeling secure I was somehow dissociated from a deeper truth, the truth of the world's suffering. It did not end with the Shoah. In recent times in Bosnia, in Kosovo, in Sierra Leone, in Northern Ireland, in Israel, in Palestine, in Iraq the legacy of what was done in the past has leapt into monstrous form. Parents tell their children what was done to their grandparents. The horror finds new ways to live and to repeat its terrible stories. As Anne Michaels puts it: "History is the poisoned well, seeping into the groundwater." And now you are back, demanding my life energy, my ear for your mutterings.

You are strong enough now, to look into the face of horror to which you were born. This is your birthright. You were born in the middle of the catastrophe, summer 1943, as your kin were being herded into cattle cars, as they forced a Rabbi to dance on the shoulders of his Yeshivah bocher, and then knocked him down. The Warsaw uprising had just been crushed. On the night of your birth

---

63 Lowinsky, *red clay is talking*, pp. 15-19.

Dresden was firebombed. You were born into a fire sign. How can you live out of your full fiery nature, if you don't face this awful history? I need you to hear my agony.

My story can't be healed. My life can't be set to rights. I need you to live in the presence of that inconsolable grief: that you were never placed into my arms when you were a baby, that I never smelt your mother's milk upon your skin, that I died among strangers, all of us ripped out of our lives, severed from friends, family, from our kitchens, our gardens, our routines, our ways of talking to God. And when I died there was no ritual, no burial, no Kaddish, no mourners, no grave, no headstone for you to put a rock on. I am a restless hungry ghost. My connection to the eternal got ripped at my death. I can't find my way home.

You who live in physical space, in the six dimensions, who eat fine food and drink good wine, who play peek-a-boo with your grandchildren and watch their eyes fill with laughing light when your face returns to their sight, you who have had time to study Kabbala, Jewish mysticism, time to read and write poetry, what can you say to me about the catastrophe and God?

I was recently in Holland, to meet a cousin I'd never heard of until she found me on the Internet. Is that what you want me to write about?

It seems only right that you would honor the names you saw inscribed in the book of the dead.

It was a powerful experience to meet a woman whose father was my father's first cousin, whose grandfather was my grandfather's brother, of whose lineage my father never spoke. We spent three days together and I saw that Lowinsky charm and intelligence in her face. We drove to Schreveningen, where you all had lived. The low Netherland landscape, the clusters of trees under the great moody vault of the sky felt so familiar, so haunting. There was a turbulence of clouds, their edges illuminated by the sun, an occasional windmill, sometimes rain. Was I reminded of Flemish painting? Or was this some sort of ancestral memory?

We sat, my cousin Sjoera, Dan and I, in the elegant old Kurhaus hotel by the North sea, drinking tea, eating little sandwiches. Did you sit here too, looking out at the view, imagining you could see England? We walked to the house my mother lived in as a teenager. We wandered through the garden where she married my father. We compared the old photograph with its glimpse of a church tower behind the brick patio. Mother looked so happy in her long gown, her veil pushed back. She held my father's arm and looked away from her own family to you and your husband. He was grinning. You looked a mixture of pleasure and pain. I think by then Grandfather was carrying on with his Bonnie, betraying you.

Sjoera told me stories of her side of the family, how her grandfather betrayed his wife as my grandfather did you, how her grandmother Rebecca died of sadness. Her son Max had been shot by the Nazis. Her grandson Grigor and his mother, whose name no one recalls, whom Max never married, were killed in a concentration camp. She spoke of Rebecca's daughter Bertha, called Beppy, taken away at age 17.

The next day we wandered around Amsterdam, through streets where you could get high off the marijuana in the air. Ladies of the night dressed in provocative lingerie showed their wares through windows. We walked on cobblestones, by canals, over bridges, through a good humored crowd. We went into the Anne Frank house, and traced her short life in exhibits and photos. At the end there was a large book, listing the names of the Dutch Jews who were killed by the Nazis. Standing with my cousin Sjoera, we looked under the "L"s. Why is it so powerful to see printed names in a book? It seemed as if everything was ripped apart and put together in that moment. This woman, with my same last name, who until day before yesterday was a total stranger, stood by me. Our arms touched, and we wept together, as we read the names of our mutual dead:

> Lowinsky, Bertha 25-12-1926 Amsterdam
>
> 30-9-1944 Sorbitor
>
> Lowinsky, Grigor 18-2-1938 Amsterdam
>
> Lowinsky, Leopold 26-9-1877 Taraschte
>
> 26-2-1943 Auschwitz
>
> Lowinsky, Max 19-2-1913 Bjela Uzeptkan

Your name wasn't there. I guess because you died of cancer. Strictly speaking, the Nazis didn't kill you. Did seeing those names in print make the stories more real? Did standing there together, two women with the same last name, bind us in family?

We left the Anne Frank house and wandered through the streets. How was it for my grandfather to put on the yellow star in 1941? His Bonnie was not Jewish. What became of her?

We wandered around the festival of culture where hip-hop and rap competed with Mozart, Rembrandt and break dancing for our attention. A naked mime covered in red clay and a loincloth mimicked us. Our ghosts were present. An angel with white wings gave away pink candy hearts. A girl twirled seven hoops of different colors around her agile body. We spoke of the dead.

Did the dead speak to you?

My grandfather, Leopold, did.

Well, what did he say?

He was mad at me, for never writing about him. He told his side of the story. He wasn't very complimentary to you.

Tell me what he said. I'm a ghost. I can handle the painful facts of my life.

He showed up laughing. I asked him what was so funny. He had had a difficult life and a terrible death. He said:

"Death isn't funny, but life is a big joke. It's all in how you look at it. It's all in the hand you're dealt. You can cry or you can laugh. My wife, Clara, she chose to cry. She became an old woman full of lamentation. I left her to her sorrow. She loved it more than she loved me. She wrapped her arms around her sorrow in the night, around her lost daughter, Maia, still in Germany, sick with TB. She wrapped her sorrow in sheets. She washed and washed those sad sheets until they were rags. She had made a little dress for our pretty granddaughter. How she wore that dress out in her endless laments and imaginings. She washed it in salt tears, in black milk. I couldn't stand it. What kind of life did she want me to stay in, among ashes, we will all be ashes soon enough I told her. What is the benefit in tears and in wailing? You take what is handed you: the yellow star, the edicts forbidding Jews entry to public places. You make what you make of it.

"I went out dancing with a young woman who smiled at me, who touched my cheek, who made me feel young and glad to be alive. I chose a long drag on a good cigarette, a roll in the hay with a willing woman. Is this such a sin? To love life? Is this why my only son shunned me and why you have made no nest for me among your writings?"

Well, it's good you gave him some space. But I suspect you are more like me than like him, that you need to feel your grief, that you cannot deny the truth of your life. That is why I keep haunting you. Leopold never could understand what I suffered. But there are those who could—they are the poets. You need to understand that the poets are your ancestors as surely as am I and Leopold.

There are poets who can help you understand what haunts you better than I can.

Black Milk

And so, in the way of ghosts, my grandmother haunts, prods, tugs me toward the Jewish poets of the Shoah, especially to the poets Nelly Sachs and Paul Celan. She wants me to understand her experience. Sachs and Celan provide her with the words.

Though Nelly Sachs and Paul Celan were of different generations, lived in different countries, and had different experiences of what Celan referred to simply as "what happened," they became important friends to one another. They met only a few times and conducted their passionate friendship primarily through letters and the exchange of poems.

Nelly Sachs was born in Berlin in 1891. She was of my grandmother's generation. Her upper-middle class parents felt thoroughly at home in Germany. John Felstiner, who is Celan's translator and biographer, said this of her experience:

> At seventeen, in love with a non-Jew, she was left by him and suffered severely . . . Her neo-Romantic verse . . . concerned Christmas and Easter, animals and landscape, Mozart, her parents . . . With the Nazi advent in 1933, Sachs turned toward Biblical themes and Hasidic mysticism . . . After 1938 she was threatened by the Gestapo; the man she still loved, now a resistance fighter, was killed before her eyes. On 16 May, 1940 she fled with her mother to Stockholm . . . and soon began translating Swedish poetry into German, meanwhile consecrating her own writing to "the suffering of Israel."[64]

Though she is little known in America these days, and her books are out of print, Sachs won the Nobel Prize for Poetry in 1966. Paul Celan, who is well known and highly regarded in American poetry circles, was born in 1920, the year my mother was born. He came from German-speaking Jewish parents and lived in Czernowitz, Bukovina, an Eastern outpost of the Austrian Empire that passed to Romania before Paul was born. He, like Sachs, was an only child, very close to his mother, and schooled in the great tradition of German poetry: Goethe, Heine, Schiller.

---

64 Paul Celan and Nelly Sachs, *Correspondence*, p. 111.

In 1941, according to Felstiner, the Romanian army and police joined the Germans in "obliterating a six-hundred-year Jewish presence: burning the Great Synagogue; imposing the yellow badge; plundering, torturing, and slaughtering community leaders and three thousand others . . ."[65] Celan and his parents escaped. But in the following year, when Celan was 22 and had had, by one account, a falling out with his father and stormed out of the house, he returned the next day to find his parents gone. They had been rounded up and deported. Paul never saw them again. His poetry is filled with the longing for his lost mother:

> Autumn bled all away, Mother, snow burned me through:
> I sought out my heart so it might weep, I found—oh the summer's
> breath,
> it was like you.
> Then came my tears . . .[66]

Leah Shelleda, in her important book on art and terror in the 20th century, *In the Shadow of its Wings* says of Celan:

> (He) will live a perpetual, inconsolable 'yahrzeit' . . . the memory of catastrophe continued to reverberate. It was not dulled by time; there was no getting over it. To recover is to betray those one had lost.[67]

This inconsolable loss is expressed in a poem by Nelly Sachs called "Chorus of the Orphans." Celan found it in a literary journal in 1953, and wrote to Sachs, beginning their intense connection. Here is part of the poem:

> We orphans
> we lament to the world:
> At night our parents play hide and seek—
> From behind the black folds of night
> Their faces gaze at us
> Their mouths speak:
> Kindling we were in a woodcutter's hand—
> . . . . .
>
> We orphans
> We lament to the world:
> Stones have become our playthings,
> Stones have faces, father and mother faces
> They wilt not like flowers, nor bite like beasts—

---

65 John Felstiner, *Paul Celan: Poet, Survivor, Jew*, pp. 12-13.
66 Celan, *Selected Poems and Prose*, p. 15.
67 Leah Shelleda, *In the Shadow of its Wings*, unpublished.

And burn not like tinder when tossed into the oven—[68]

My grandmother's ghost feelings are voiced in this poem. She too was orphaned: she lost her God, her home, her past, her future, her children, her grandchildren. And suddenly, listening to her suffering in Sachs' powerful imagery, I find myself beset by that difficult old question, one I've been protected from by the firewall I've put between me and the Shoah, a question raised in the 1950s by the philosopher Theodore Adorno: Is it barbaric to write poetry after Auschwitz? Does it make "an unimaginable fate"[69] somehow meaningful? Does it release us too easily from the horror? My grandmother's voice leaps to respond:

The poets give voice to the unthinkable, the unbearable, they give sorrow a voice, and lamentation. If there were only silence, song frozen by the horror, who would remember, who would mourn? Who would make wicked jokes, with "wild, cunning words" to resist the "crassness of the economic–miraculous"[70] Germany as did Paul Celan in the early 1960s? Who would remember the moment of my death? How it felt. Who was there. Who wasn't . . . God was supposed to be there when I died. No one was there. We all disappeared like smoke in the air. So says Celan, so says Sachs.

My grandmother is referring to the image of smoke both Celan and Sachs used, before they knew one another's work. Celan wrote a poem in 1946, "Todesfugue" or "Deathfugue" which became famous for its evocation of the horror of the death camps. Here is a section:

> Black milk of daybreak we drink you at night
> we drink you at midday and morning we drink you at evening
> we drink and we drink
> a man lives in the house your goldenes Haar Margareta
> your aschenes Haar Shulamith he plays with his vipers
>
> He shouts play death more sweetly this Death is a master from
> Deutschland
> he shouts scrape your strings darker you'll rise up as smoke to the sky[71]

---

68   Sachs, *O the Chimneys*, p. 29.
69   Felstiner, *Paul Celan: Poet, Survivor, Jew*, p. 188.
70   *Paul Celan: Poet, Survivor, Jew*, p. 191.
71   Celan, *Selected Poetry and Prose*, pp. 31-32.

My grandmother is rocking her ghost body in me, weeping, tearing her hair. The poem shouts her horror: the madness, the dance of death going faster and faster while the master from Deutschland, who loves music and high culture, evokes the Margareta of Goethe's Faust and the Shulamith of the Song of Songs whose hair is of ashes, in crazy company with vipers. If the poets don't say how it was, who will?

Nelly Sachs' poem is called "O the Chimneys" which became the title of her "Selected Poems." The poem has an epigraph from Job. Here is part of it.

And though after my skin worms destroy this body, yet in my flesh shall I see God—

O the chimneys!
Freedomway for Jeremiah and Job's dust—
Who devised you and laid stone upon stone
The road for refugees of smoke?

O the habitations of death,
Invitingly appointed
for the host who used to be a guest—
O you fingers
Laying the threshold
Like a knife between life and death—

O you chimneys,
O you fingers
And Israel's body as smoke through the air![72]

My grandmother's ghost breath settles down in my body. She rests in me. The poem orients her. It is at once lamentation and accusation: "the host who used to be a guest" is the human who takes the power of a god into his hands. To be part of Israel's body as smoke through the air is, strangely, consolation for a ghost.

We wonder, this ghost and her granddaughter, about Sachs' choice of that section of Job, "yet in my flesh shall I see God"? We muse about Sachs as a religious poet. It was her goal, her longing, to see God. Celan believed she did, and that in her company, he too caught a glimpse. This happened in May, 1960, when, after many years of corresponding, the two poets met for the first time. Sachs was to receive the Droste prize in Germany. Though it

---

72 Sachs, *O the Chimneys*, p. 3.

had been 20 years since she fled she still could not bear to stay overnight in Germany and so met Celan in Zürich.[73] Celan wrote a poem about this meeting, "Zürich, at the Stork", and dedicated it to Nelly Sachs:

> On the day of an ascension, the
> Minster stood . . . over there, it came
> with some gold across the water.
>
> Our talk was of your God, I spoke
> against him . . .[74]

Celan was referring to the day of Christ's ascension into heaven, and to the sight of Zürich's great church reflected in the river. Both poets were steeped in Jewish mysticism, both had read Gershom Sholem's translation of the Zohar. They understood the sacred meaning of light in the Kabbalistic tradition. Celan credited Sachs with showing him this light. She was a Jewish mystic with a deep connection to the sacred alphabet. She writes in a poem:

> Then wrote the scribe of *the Sohar*
> opening the words' mesh of veins
> instilling blood from stars . . .
>
> The alphabet's corpse rose from the grave,
> alphabet angel, ancient crystal . . .[75]

Writing was Sachs' way to the divine, but she did not have an easy relationship with her God. Neither did Celan. Though he claimed not to be a believer many of his strongest poems wrestle directly with God. Both poets were beleaguered by darkness and psychological pain. Sachs suffered from a persecution mania that had a basis in reality. There was a Nazi revival in Sweden in the late 1950s. However her paranoia extended to the noise from the water pipes in her apartment, and she was hospitalized several times in her later life. Celan suffered from dark depressions and was also frequently hospitalized.

We wonder, the ghost of my grandmother and I, whether they were really crazy, or whether they were carrying the unbearable burden of their times, trying to digest what could not be digested. Were they, as poets, more perme-

---

73   Felstiner, *Paul Celan: Poet, Survivor, Jew*, p. 156.
74   Celan, *Selected Poems and Prose*, p. 141.
75   Sachs, *O the Chimneys*, p. 123.

able than others to the horror? It was their job to give sorrow a voice, lamentation words to say, their job to find images for the unthinkable. They were carrying something for us all. It was simply too much. Listen to Nelly Sachs:

> This is the landscape of screams!
> Ascension made of screams
> out of the bodies grate of bones . . .
>
> Job's scream to the four winds....
>
> O you bleeding eye
> in the tattered eclipse of the sun
> hung up to be dried by God . . .[76]

Hers is no Christian God of goodness and kindness. Neither is the God whom Celan addresses in his powerful poem, "Tenebrae." The title refers to a Catholic service during which candles are extinguished to symbolize the Crucifixion. A gospel portion is read: "Tenebrae factae sunt"—"there was darkness over the earth".

> Near are we, Lord,
> near and graspable.
>
> Grasped already, Lord,
> clawed into each other, as if
>
> each of our bodies were
> your body, Lord.
>
> Pray Lord,
> pray to us,
> we are near.[77]

The poem makes a clear, unbearable allusion to the manner in which people died in the gas ovens of the Shoah. Anne Michaels gives us a prose version:

When they opened the doors, the bodies were always in the same position. Compressed against one wall, a pyramid of flesh. Still hope. The climb to

---

76 Sachs, *O the Chimneys* p. 129.
77 Celan, *Selected Poems and Prose*, p. 103.

air, to the last disappearing pocket of breath near the ceiling. The terrifying hope of human cells.[78]

The poem stands the whole idea of prayer on its head. God is supposed to pray to us. Our bodies, clawed unto each other in a terrible death, are God's body. Is Celan saying that we suffering mortals are morally superior to God, that God needs us humans to express the terrible aspect of the divine?

My ghost grandmother is making a loud noise in my heart as we read Sachs and Celan. It excites her to notice that certain themes seem to come directly from those poets, appear in my poems, before I ever read them. It is as though they were floating about in the cultural unconscious, as though I was drawing from my poetic lineage before I knew of it consciously. For example in my poem called "*Hera Reflects on the Anniversary of a Long Ago Dissolved First Marriage*" there is a passage explaining the pressure I felt to have children young:

> all those ghosts
> fresh out
> of the ovens
> fresh out of
> mass graves
> they had
> no stones
> to lay down their heads
> no baskets
> for their bones
> no ground
> for their roots
> they spilled over
> oceans
> invading
> demanding
> new born
> baby
> bodies—[79]

Sachs has a poem called "Chorus of the Unborn." Here is a section:

> Listen, you who are sick with parting:
> We are those who begin to live in your glances,

---

78 Michaels, *Fugitive Pieces*, p. 168.
79 Lowinsky, *red clay is talking*, p. 41.

In your hands which are searching the blue air—
We are those who smell of morning.
Already your breath is inhaling us,
Drawing us down into your sleep
Into the dreams which are our earth...[80]

"She's talking," says the ghost of my grandmother, "about you, your whole generation. And she's talking, as were you, about the powerful push for new life after so much death."

Celan wrote of poetry as "something standing open, occupiable, perhaps toward an addressable Thou." I was possessed by this notion of an addressable you, before I had ever read Celan's poem, "Radix, Matrix."

As one speaks to stone, as
you,
to me from the abyss, from
a homeland con-
Sanguined, up–
Hurled, you,
you of old to me,
you in the Nix of a night to me,
you in Yet-Night en-
Countered, you
Yet–You—:[81]

My poem entitled "you" repeats the word "you" with an urgency that seems straight out of Celan. Here is the last part of the poem:

you
break into my night—
rattle my rib cage—
make biblical claims
        on my flesh—

        you
        two a.m. terror
        lusting for what
                        you have made—
        lord of the apple tree—

        angel with fangs—

80 Sachs, *O the Chimneys*, p. 43.
81 Celan, *Selected Poems and Prose*, p. 167.

i spit like an old jewish woman
water to dust
in your hands—

suddenly everything's

fire
on the mountain—

you—

burning
in me—

never
consumed[82]

So, it appears that I was in receipt of a poetic legacy before having read it. As the ghost of my grandmother pushed and prodded me toward Sachs and Celan, I began to understand that I had kin in poetry who had much to teach me about what haunts me. Did these poets work out a relationship to their terror? I think they did in the only way my grandmother's ghost can understand—to know it as an aspect of divinity. To wrestle with God is not to repudiate or to deny the divine. It is a form of relationship to it. Sachs and Celan grasp this, informed by Jewish mysticism and the Kabbala. In the rich hermetic tradition of Jewish mysticism, as it is expressed in the glyph of the Tree of Life, the lightening flash of God's ineffable being is traced from its most unknown and unsayable to its most touchable reality—our human realm. It passes from masculine to feminine and back, from severity to compassion, from energy to form. God becomes human, and we humans are a part of God.

The indwelling of the Shekinah, the feminine face of God, is both process and goal of the journey down to the ground of manifestation and back up to the mystery of mysteries. This is the God who is revealed to the poet, the mystic, the ecstatic. To honor such a God is not to be protected from evil, from terror, from suffering. It is to expand our sense of the holy. It is to follow within oneself the trajectory of light, as did Nelly Sachs, as did Paul Celan. In his poem, "Psalm," Celan writes:

No one kneads us again
out of earth and clay

---

82 Lowinsky, *red clay is talking*, p. 138.

no one incants our dust.
No one.

Blessed art thou, No One.
In thy sight would
we bloom
In thy
spite.[83]

To wrestle with God as "No One" is a mystical idea. It also expresses the despair of those who got no help from God in the catastrophe. The "No One" who was there at my grandmother Clara's death is transformed by Celan's blazingly simple phrase combining the opposite faces of God: "Blessed art thou, No One."

Sachs prefigures the return of the religious attitude in the Goddess religions, which will flood the western psyche soon after her death, in simple, powerful images that are the essence of the Shekinah:

Like a milkmaid
at dusk
your fingertips pull
at the hidden sources
of light....

Dancer
woman in childbirth
you alone
carry on the hidden navel-string
of your body
the identical god-given jewels
of death and birth.[84]

Both Sachs and Celan were often plunged into darkness—their own, their peoples, their times. Both struggled, in their poems, to find their way back to the light. When Celan was in the psychiatric clinic he had shock therapy, and read Freud. As far as I know he had no psychotherapy. But he read Gershom Sholem on the Kabbala. And, according to his biographer, in a moment of despair, he wrote out one of the sacred names of God in Judaism: "Shaddai! Shaddai!" That something transformative happened to him in his encounter

---

83 Celan, *Selected Poems and Prose*, p. 157.
84 Sachs, *O the Chimneys*, p. 159.

with the Kabbala is made evident by a poem he wrote while still in the hospital: "Nah, am Aortenbogen" or "Near, in the aorta's arch." It is such a short poem I will quote it in its entirety:

> Near, in the aorta's arch,
> in brightblood
> the brightword.
>
> Mother Rachel
> weeps no more.
> Carried across now
> all of the weeping.
>
> Still, in the coronary arteries,
> unbinded:
>
> Ziv, that light.[85]

Celan moves from the physiology of human blood flow, (certainly an image of how God manifests in human form), to the tragic history of the Jews, "Mother Rachel weeps no more" to a Hebrew word Gershom Sholem ascribed to the indwelling light of the Shekinah: "Ziv."[86] This, his biographer believes, is a word he has been waiting for and that has been waiting for him, a word for the light he saw when he was in Zürich with Nelly Sachs, and again, when Nelly visited him and his family in Paris, a word for the mystery.

To find a way to move from the aorta's arch to the light, a way to translate mystical experience, does not, it appears, necessarily resolve one's own agony. At age 50, Celan took his life, jumped into the Seine. But not before he had written his last message to Nelly Sachs, who represented for him his lost mother, and the sister he never had: "all gladness dear Nelly, all light!" He tried so hard to pull her out of her darkness, when he himself was drowning in his own. She had written him: "the net of fear and terror that they threw over me hasn't yet been raised."[87] And Celan answers: "I think of you Nelly, always . . . Do you still remember, when we spoke for the second time of God, in our house . . . how a golden light shimmered on the wall? Through you, through your nearness, such things become visible . . . Look Nelly: the net

---

85　Celan, *Selected Poems and Prose*, p. 303.
86　Felstiner, *Paul Celan: Poet, Survivor, Jew*, p. 239.
87　Paul Celan and Nelly Sachs, *Correspondence*, p. 35.

is being drawn away! . . . Look, it is getting light, you are breathing, you are breathing freely. You will not be lost to us . . ."[88]

He is saying an incantation, to try to keep her among the living, which he could not do for his mother, or even, it seems, for himself. Sachs died of cancer on the day Celan was buried.

You don't need a family connection to the Shoah to be haunted by troubling ghosts. We all feel them in our bones these days—whether they were ripped out of their lives in lower Manhattan on Sept. 11, disappeared in Chile and Argentina, blown up in a house in Ramallah, a street in Baghdad, torn out of a village in Sierra Leone or Bosnia. So many taken violently, shockingly out their lives. They wail, they keen, they mutter warnings. The ghosts want our attention.

And when you pay attention to ghosts, acknowledge terror, look horror in the face, it changes one. My grandmother is shifting in me. She is going from ghost to light, from fearful presence one does not want to face to a bright, fierce energy. She is a firebrand. She is a burning bush. She comes to me as clarity, for her name is Clara. She has pushed me to wrestle with God in my poetry. She tells me that for now she is satisfied with me, but she wants me to end this chapter with a recent poem of mine, written to her, and, at her request, called "muse".

muse

grandmother

      have you been released out of the realm of the moon
         has your spirit risen to the sun's
            place of sacrifice
            are you speaking to me
                from there
                              grandmother?

  have you leapt
           the abyss
              do you see
                  the unseen?

---

88   Celan and Sachs, *Correspondence*, p. 36.

are you known to the one?
are you one with me?
do i breathe you dream you pray you
draw you down to my life every
morning?

grandmother goblet
catcher of ecstasy
maker of forms
Sofia of the kingdom

worlds are created
you tell me

worlds
are destroyed[89]

---

89 Lowinsky, *a maze*, p. 8.

Old Mother India

We . . . have to follow the difficult way of our own experiences, produce our own reactions, and assimilate our own sufferings and realizations. Only then will the truth that we bring to manifestation be . . . our own flesh and blood . . . We cannot borrow God . . . Divinity must descend . . . into the matter of our own existence . . .

—Heinrich Zimmer[90]

Nina in Progress

Though we are all shaped by the fate of our families and the dead that haunt us, we also have our own particular destiny. Mine took me in unexpected directions. The image I had when I was a young woman, of who I would become, never materialized. I had no way of knowing then that my Muse was plotting an entirely different path for me. Who I was becoming was a dark glimmering, a stirring in unconscious waters, while I was blithely making other plans. For example, in my early twenties, married, with children, I thought I knew who I was becoming when I left graduate school in English Literature. I didn't want to write footnotes. I was to be a novelist. I had in fact begun one, a bildungsroman, so I thought, about a self-conscious young woman in the Berkeley of the early 60s. I called her Nina—"Nina in Progress." Wrong. My Muse did not visit me, while I wrestled with Nina, who was never completed. I never became that novelist. My Muse had other plans. I was to meet her in her manifestation as Mother India. Looking back at that young woman I was, younger than my youngest child is now, the sheer clairvoyance of my destiny takes my breath away.

At the time it seemed more like being dragged along in the undertow of other people's destinies. I had not signed up for this. India scared me. I was caught up in the fate of the young men of my generation for whom the Vietnam war burned hellishly at the periphery of consciousness, threatening death raids on life plans. My then husband was threatened. As a young doctor he would be drafted into the medical corps, unless he signed up for some other service, such as Peace Corps.

---

90 Heinrich Zimmer, *Philosophies of India*, p. 2.

"Sure" I said, "Peace Corps would be interesting." I had an image of a North African city. Was it Casablanca I was hoping for, the romance of Bogart and Bergman? Certainly not India.

At the time it seemed to us that going to India had to do with Lyndon Johnson's fate. His presidency was haunted by the popularity of his assassinated predecessor, Jack Kennedy. Johnson, in competition with a ghost, enlarged the Kennedy initiated Peace Corps and sent hordes of volunteers to India. Such a horde required support staff, like Peace Corps doctors, which is what my husband became. I got carried along on this wave of young Americans that entered India in the mid 1960s, and soon ebbed away, because no one was quite sure what to do with all of us. And anyway, in India you have to create relationships, drink tea and socialize with the appropriate officials, before you can begin to do anything, and by then it's almost time to turn around again and come home.

But, I am getting ahead of my story. I want to give you a picture of the young woman I was: twenty-four years old, in the short skirts and long straight hair of the era, a baby daughter in my arms and a four year old son by my side, seventeen pieces of luggage and a husband, luckily, grounded enough to keep track of all that, and our tickets. It is 2 a.m. London time and we have just arrived at Heathrow Airport. Something has gone wrong with our hotel reservations. I can't remember what we did with all that luggage but I do remember walking the streets in an exhausted haze, holding the baby, looking for a place to stay. A bed and breakfast took us in and we learned about the gray density of British porridge the next morning.

It was 1967. A trip to Picadilly Circus showed us a London throbbing with Beatles music, mini skirts, colors as vibrant as the yellow submarine, a joyous feeling of new life and possibility. It was the same summer the flower children arrived in the Haight Ashbury. But we were not destined to know the late 1960s of London or San Francisco. India was waiting for us.

Years later I would come to understand what was about to happen to me. In the language of the 60s, my mind was about to be blown, for the way we organize experience in the west gets disorganized in India. The splits that are familiar to western thought are not found in Indian philosophy or religion. In Hinduism, I learned, there is no beginning and no end. As in Indian music, creation, expansion and destruction, the realms of Bhrahma, Vishnu and Shiva, are phases of a rhythmic process that goes on and on. The split between monotheism and polytheism does not exist in Hinduism. There are many gods in human forms, in animal forms, we see them wherever we look: Shiva, Shakti, Vishnu, Lakshmi, Hanuman the monkey god, Ganesha the god with an elephant head. And, at the same time all these gods are the manifestation of the one god, Brahman, who has no particular shape but is manifest in everything that is. The famous Bengali poet Rabindranath Tagore expressed this beautifully in "Gitanjali."

> The same stream of life that runs through my veins night and day runs through the world and dances in rhythmic measures. It is the same life that shoots in joy through the dust of the earth in numberless blades of grass and breaks into tumultous waves of leaves and flowers. It is the same life that is rocked in the ocean—cradle of birth and death, in ebb and in flow. I feel my limbs are made glorious by the touch of this world of life. And my pride is from the life-throb of ages dancing in my blood this moment.[91]

In Hinduism there is no first cause, no big Bang, no god as author of the universe, as in western thought. "Who has seen the first born, when he that had no bones bore him that has bones?"[92] cries the Vedic seer. The belief that Brahman lives in every being, human, animal, plant, rock, fills the Indian landscape with a living divinity. There is something hypnotic about it, as though to enter that culture is to go into a trance. My Muse touched me with that 'life-throb of ages' and I have never been the same.

Imagine then, a young woman, in 1967, with a baby in her arms and a four year old by the hand, entering this altered state of consciousness. She has studied western literature, read T.S. Eliot and William Carlos Williams, Walt Whitman, Emily Dickinson. Nothing prepared her for this.

Imagine her arriving in Delhi on a dark steamy night. It is raining. As the little family walks down the staircase of the airplane a row of dark skinny men with knobby knees in huge khaki shorts hold umbrellas over their heads. They are creating a covered walkway for them to enter the tiny terminal. It seems to her an extravagant act of gallantry. Imagine the biggest beetle you have ever seen crossing her path in that terminal, promising snakes and scorpions. Imagine the outstretched palms of a thousand beggars standing outside her hotel room window in her dream that first night. At breakfast the next morning, her son, drinking orange juice, takes a bite out of the thin glass. "Hold your mouth open! Don't swallow! Don't move" his frightened

---

91 Rabindranath Tagore, *A Tagore Reader*, p. 305.
92 Swami Prabhavananda, *The Spiritual Heritage of India*, p. 33.

father is shouting, pulling pieces of glass out of his mouth. India is marvelous, fearful, monstrous.

Imagine the young family arriving at the airport in Hyderabad, in South India, where they are to live for two years. They are greeted by a crowd of Americans, mostly Peace Corps, some expatriate. They are garlanded with jasmine and pummeled with questions: "What music have you brought? The lastest Beatles album? The new Jefferson Airplane?" The women want to see her clothes. Indian tailors can copy anything. Imagine her new jumpsuit, bought in a moment of fashion bravura, on all the American women in Hyderabad in many colors of Indian silk and cotton. This will be the only time in her life she starts a fashion trend.

In bureaucratese I was what was ungraciously known as a "non-matrix spouse." I continued to consider myself a novelist. Everyday I spent a few hours on Nina's progress. Perhaps I was holding onto my western consciousness, sitting in the spicy trance of India, imagining the streets of Berkeley.

We opened our house in Hyderabad to Peace Corps volunteers. There was always someone sleeping on the floor, always several of us around the dining room table talking American politics, Indian politics, philosophies of life. We were there when Martin Luther King was assassinated. We were there when Robert Kennedy was assassinated.

India held us young Americans with curiosity and compassion and deep kindness. She mourned our fallen leaders with us. Sheela, who washed my floors every morning, and sat in the kitchen deftly removing rocks one by one from our daily rice, had lost three of her five children. She asked me about Rose Kennedy—how many sons had she lost. Three I told her—one in the war, two by assassination. "Abah! Three grown sons!" And she wept with me. She told me she had a photograph of JFK in her home, next to her photograph of Mahatma Ghandi. Now she would add photographs of RFK and MLK.

Mother India

India joined us, seduced us, absorbed us, changed us in ways not entirely visible to us. The West of me says, "That's culture shock. India took you out of your cultural habits of mind, your unconscious rigidities, everything you thought you knew came into question. It opened you up to the archetypal realm. What to do after that but become a Jungian?"

The East of me says: *You caught a glimpse of your deepest self here in India. Why else would you adopt an Indian child? You were a Hindu in a former life. Your karma and hers have been intertwined for many lifetimes.*

For most of the last thirty years the West of me has been dominant. I've done the work of young and middle adulthood: raised a family, developed a profession. I've done it in the manner of my culture and my generation, which has struggled with the roles of men and women. Like many others I got divorced, spent many years as a single mother, and then remarried, doing the work of creating a stepfamily.

But all through those years, I told my youngest, my Indian daughter, that when she was ready, if she wanted me to, I'd take her to India. This promise seemed a long way off. It would be years before she'd be ready. I would have passed the noon of my life and moved into the afternoon. She had struggled with her sense of direction in her late teens, in her twenties. She had dropped out of college.

She had a dream of two elephants. She said they were her birth mother and her adoptive mother. She had a dream in which she fell, and an Indian woman in a sapphire blue sari, gave her a look which said: pick yourself up and go live your life. She did. She went back to school. She became a re-entry woman at Mills College. She studied Indian art. At Mills she found her voice. And it became clear to me, and to her stepfather, that she was ready for India.

And so it was that one night in January, some years ago, Shanti, Dan and I landed in Mumbai and my Muse in her eastern manifestation began to reassert herself. She had been waiting, she told me, for thirty years, maybe thirty lifetimes. She has always been there, even when I forgot her. She revealed herself in a poem I wrote for Shanti before we left. I was astonished at how clearly my inner eye saw her. This is the poem:

we return to mother India

for Shanti

there will be a commotion
when we arrive
there always is
a crowd and a confusion
dark eyes

open palms
bony children
tribal women
silver jewelry
skirts of red and orange and purple cloth with mirrors
beggars swooping down like birds to touch our feet

paise amah amah amah paise

there is always an elephant kneeling to receive a rider
there is always a cow dung patty
being slapped into shape
to dry on a wall
to be fuel for the fire cooking idli and sambhar for breakfast

there is always a white cow
hipbones protruding
who has laid herself down for a rest in the middle of traffic
rickshaw wallahs are shouting
lorry drivers are honking
a brahmin in a dhoti is slapping her sacred hide

there is always a god
stepping out of the stone
there is always a dream bleeding through into day

we come from the west
amaji
old mother
I bring you my daughter
she is your daughter—

what do your dark eyes remember of me

who came to you young
full of milk and children
drunk on the manifestation of things
you taught me your dance
with naked feet slapping the heat of the earth
you taught me to carry my baby on my hip
to wrap my sari low and tight
to pound cumin seed on a stone
to cook red chillis in hot oil
until the smell comes

what did your dark eyes see
of this daughter's birth
mother
was she beautiful?
did she sneak out of her married bed
to join her lover in the jasmine scented night?
did her heart moan like a grieving elephant
when she handed her girlchild over?

amaji
old mother
which one of us swallowed the other?
did you enter my bloodstream
feed essence of rasa through me to your daughter
though i left you many years ago
the east of me never stopped wandering

your labyrinth
dark streets
bright bazaars
secret corners
temples
stupas

did you crack my skull open
like a betel nut
chewing the west of me
in your red stained teeth and spitting out
the shells
to make me a mother
for this daughter of yours?
does she look like her birth

mother
does she look like the soul of her country
does she look like the village women
who carry a basket of rocks on their heads
and build houses?

she is well educated
she has studied your art
she has seen Krishna dancing
on the walls of her house
two elephant mothers have met
in her dreams

old mother
amaji
i am bringing you our daughter
for a blessing
we are feeding milk to the gods
we are throwing jasmine petals in the river
we are bowing down and touching

the soles of your feet[93]

I had many fears approaching old mother India with my daughter and my second husband who had never been there before. I was afraid Shanti would not be accepted as an Indian, as a Hindu. I was afraid of India, its chaos, its poverty, its population growth, its AIDS epidemic, its terrible suffering. But the old mother wrapped us in her magic, her generosity, her open hearted devotion. She spun us a tale of synchronicity and blessings. Archetypal themes unfolded. A trail of elephants guided us. Shanti was accepted, wrapped in gorgeous saris. A woman like the woman in her dream appeared. Marvels happened. We dreamt of rainbows. And then it was over. We were back in the U.S. of A.

It was as if the gods had been bled out of the sky. Bereft of the landscape teeming with sacred images, dancing Ganeshas, purple and gold lions and peacocks embroidered on the saris of the women breaking up rocks on the road, temples teeming with divinities and in every pasture, a shrine.

Now we were sitting in an airport van with no god on the dashboard, no yellow and orange marigolds garlanding the windshield, no incense holder,

---

93 Lowinsky, *red clay is talking*, p. 67.

no white bullocks with yellow and blue painted horns, no lorries with gold and blue tinsel and the name of a god whose company they represent: Krishna travels, Lakshmi Goods Carrier, Shakti Motors, Jagannath Distributers; no brown cow lying, head tilted upward in deep contemplation in the middle of the traffic island; no white cow urinating a golden stream in front of the medical supply store, no chaos of rickshaws, motorscooters, motorcycles, bicycles with baskets carrying bananas, white hens with red combs, notebooks.

We were home and the sky was pale blue—empty eyes in a concrete world. Someone had stolen my hand luggage at the San Francisco airport. In it was my notebook, with an image of the tree of life on its cover. I had written in it every day of our journey. Lost. Lost also the necklace of silver chains Dan had bought for me in Hyderabad and the garnet pendant he had given me early in our marriage. I never got them back. All through India we had worried about our luggage being stolen. Everywhere, in ways we often did not understand, people took care of us. They took us in directions we had not asked to go, and we found ourselves exactly where we needed to be.

Elephant Blessing

This time I can't afford to lose what India has given me. It is the afternoon of my life and I need my Hindu side. I call upon the East of me, I invoke her. She's come in poetry. She was so familiar in India. Maybe I can get her back, even at home, in the U.S. of A. She appears, as though she has always been there. And indeed, I recognize her from dreams, from poems, from active imagination. She is dark skinned, and wears a deep red sari and a brass belt around her waist. Once, in a dream, she tucked me into bed. Once in active imagination, she spoke to me of the connection between the erotic and the sacred. She has long dark Indian eyes, like my daughter, Shanti. I ask her who she is:

I have many names. All of them are true. None of them are true. Some call me Vac, goddess of the language that flames up to the gods when the sacrifice is lit; daughter of Ritual-Skill, wife of Vision, Mother of emotions.

Some call me Lila, I am the divine play between the gods and the humans.

Some call me Shakti, I am the energy that gives form to the world, the yoni embracing Shiva's lingam.[94]

Some call me Sarasvati, the flowing one, she who is wise, mother of poetry. I teach humans how to bring the unbounded into a form.

Some call me Parvati, Lady of the Mountain, Daughter of the Snow Capped one, conscious substance of the universe.

Some call me Wanton eyed, Her very name is Lust, Pearl-eared, Recognizable from her Lotus.

Some call me fierce, tawny-dark, Red toothed, Mother of the God of War.

Some call me Riding on a Lion, Destroyer of the Buffalo Demon, Adorned with skulls.

I speak to you of ecstasy. I speak to you of devotion, we call it Bhakti. I speak to you of the rasas, the feeling tones, the essential juices of artistic expression: the erotic, comic, pathetic, furious, heroic, terrible, odious, marvellous and peaceful. I speak to you in poetry. I speak to you in stone carvings. I speak to you in animals and plants. I speak to you in the longing of your soul for my land. Longing is the beginning of lyric poetry. I fill you with fire. You were "born from fire... and cooked" in the womb. Mastery of fire sparked the beginnings of settledness and civilization. At the center of the home, fire transforms the raw into the cooked."[95] *I fill you with the fire of who you most deeply are.*

Listen to this song of the South Indian artist:

> *All of me is on fire,*
> *My voice, my body, my hands!*
> *I tremble with the need to express.*
> *Out of the earth I celebrate,*
> *Out of the skies comes my answer.*
> *Out of the earth I create his body,*
> *Out of space his abode.*
> *this bounty and this beauty is my source;*
> *My body is the instrument of my expressions.*[96]

In the West you think the unconscious is inside you. In the East we know it is all around us. We are in it. The divine is everywhere. That is what wrapped you up and carried you along in India. This is what came to you in the poem

---

94 Alain Danièlou, *The Myths and Gods of India*, p, 254.
95 Alistair Shearer, *The Hindu Vision*, p. 27.
96 Shearer, *The Hindu Vision*, p. 23.

you wrote before you returned to India. The elephant appeared in the poem. The elephant appeared again in front of your hotel in Bangkok, on the way to India. There was a shrine, crowded with all sorts of little elephants, brass, wood, incense, flowers. Shanti complained she had nothing to wear to enter India. You bought her a sarong, with elephants marching all around it.

At the thieves market, in Bombay, when you were all reeling with the crowds, the poverty, the beggars who would stick their crippled limbs in the car and demand alms, the pollution, the endless traffic jam, Shanti spotted that dancing Ganesha that is now your kitchen god, standing on the window sill above your sink. It is this divinity in everything you must remember, you must find words to express. This requires a sacrifice of your ordinary western consciousness This requires devotion, and that kind of ecstasy that Allan Watts described as ek-stasis, meaning to stand outside, to be liberated from the bondage of one's ego, one's personality, one's role. In ecstasy one is no longer . . . a thing or being - alone and separate from the total energy of the world.[97] *Ekstasis expresses the deepest mystery of the Self: when you lose yourself, you find yourself. You lost your notebook. But Shanti kept a notebook. Shanti made a copy of her story for you, to fill in for your lost notebook. She called it "My India." Maybe she'll fill in for you here, read how it was for her that first morning in Bombay:*

5:45 AM Monday

Bombay 1/6/97

I can't sleep at all. I've been up since 3:45 or so . . . filled with the images of the street people. I thought I was prepared for it, but I was really upset by it.

Rows and rows of people, young kids, old people, skinny men and women all in tent-type things on the sides of the road . . . Despite the extreme poverty, and filth on the streets, the women still look beautiful in the saris they wear . . . I was especially taken by the . . . children I saw living on the streets. The kids were so little. One group in particular was playing on this large A-frame looking wooden ramp; it looked like they were being regular kids, but they had no home. How do they eat? Do they know who their mommies are? Does any one tuck them in at night like my mom did (and still does)?

The other thing that really got me was how dirty the streets are. I feel like such an awful westerner. I don't think all of the filth, poverty, crowdedness are bad things. I'm just realizing how little I really know of India. I know a great deal about art, history, Hinduism, things you can study. But now I can

97 Alan Watts, *Erotic Spirituality: The Vision of Konarak*, p. 73.

really understand that India is an <u>experience!</u> It means so much to me to be able to experience it . . . the smells, the sounds of the language, the crowds, the hotel aesthetic, everything is a deeply felt experience. Like right now I can hear these savage sounding birds outside. I think they live in the tree outside my hotel window. Even the crow from these birds is different . . .

I remember those birds—Indian crows, grey hooded, sharp beaked, and, as Shanti says, savage sounding. That was the morning Shanti walked out into the streets of Mumbai (Bombay) and realized that the "street people" were not who she thought they were. They turned out to be vendors, who sold goods on the street. They had much more than she had realized when we drove by them, sleeping, in the night.

Was that the day our friends took us sari shopping? And the men, for it is men who sell saris in the elegant stores, took such pleasure in throwing out the glorious yards of silk and georgette in red and purples and greens and blacks with gold and silver embossed designs for Shanti to feel, to try on. What pleasure they took in wrapping her in sari after sari, and she would emerge, bringing tears to all of our eyes, looking so radiant, so beautiful, so Indian. These men were initiating her into the ways of the women of her birth culture. They welcomed her. They honored her. They showed her how to wrap a sari. In her words: "Boy was I a princess!"

The goddess of many names is nudging me. *Now you're back in India,* she says. *But you've forgotten our elephant theme. Tell the rest of the elephant story.*

Oh, that is the thread we were following. After we had been to Ajanta and Ellora, with our Muslim driver who said: "God is Great!" when we agreed to his fee; after we had seen the ancient frescoes painted in dark caves, telling the story of Buddha's mother, who, on the night she conceived him, dreamt a white elephant pierced her; after seeing the great elephant of the Kailasanatha at Ellora, and the demon Ravana shaking the sacred mountain, we left the west side of India and flew to Chennai. There we were met by a friend-of-a-friend, who invited us to join him at a harvest festival the next day.

Our friend, it turned out, was a member of the Lion's Club of Chennai, the same Lion's Club that business people belong to in this country. As here, they band together to network and do good works. They sponsor a blood bank which is essential to help fight the AIDS epidemic. For the first time this group had decided it would celebrate Pongol, the traditional village harvest festival. They felt too far removed from their village roots, and wanted to recreate a connection with the sacred cycle of the villages.

When we arrived at the festival the next day, Shanti looked gorgeous in her brand new red and yellow tie-dyed sari. We were greeted by the sight of a beautiful dark elephant wearing a blanket with the words "Lion's Club of Kelly" emblazoned in gold upon it. We never did figure out where Kelly was. But we were pushed toward the great beast immediately and told: "Come come, the elephant must bless you!" How does an elephant bless you? We learned that the elephant raises her trunk and brings it softly down upon the crown of your head. But, Shanti will tell it in her words:

> Everyone rushed to greet the Americans, (Mommy and Dan) and quickly brought us to the elephant to be blessed. Oh what a feeling that was. First, the decorated elephant blessed Dan, then Mommy and then me—by taking her trunk and kissing my face (I was supposed to bend my head down so she could do the back of my head instead of my face). But, I had no idea what I was supposed to do.
>
> Anyways, then we ate breakfast on banana leaves in a big room where everyone sat in rows. And the servers came by with buckets and slopped the food on our plates. The food was delicious.
>
> When we went back outside there was a Brahmin priest doing a Pongol ceremony. The priest was so old—missing teeth, very little hair, skinny, frail. He was chanting something which went along with the ceremony for Pongol. The women made a fire while he chanted and set up a pot of milk to boil. Meanwhile, while the milk was warming up the elephant came over to bless the governing officials of the Lion's Club. I wanted so badly to be blessed again, I went over and asked, "May I?" And the elephant blessed me again. It feels very significant to me that I was blessed twice by the elephant—once for each of my mothers. The second blessing was incredible. The elephant massaged the back of my head. The priest blessed me and gave me a flower garland . . . It is amazing how gentle and sturdy and present the elephant was . . . So I've been blessed in south India by the elephant goddess . . .
>
> So the milk is heating up. Music is playing and everyone is gathering around watching, anticipating the over flow of milk. It has a very sexual, climactic, orgasmic tension to the whole ceremony. Mommy thinks it's birth. I think it's sex. It's both birth and sex. Finally the milk overflows and comes pouring over the top of the pot and all the women rush to put rice in it. The whole ceremony means it will be an auspicious year.

I wrote a poem about that experience:

elephant blessing

and the elephant looked at the small human face
and saw where the feared lived
hanging from the rafters of that high pitched

                                human mind

it worried and wailed
about death
and not enough
money
love
work
fame
time
dreams

a hindu will tell you
an elephant's heart is bigger
than a human brain
that the touch of an elephant
is as close as we get
to a god

and the elephant put her sensitive trunk
down firmly
where the soft spot had long ago
been open
to the gods
and she found herself
a small human
in the middle
of a harvest festival

the drummers were drumming
the dancers were dancing
a brahmin was chanting
flowers had been offered
coconuts and bananas
milk was being heated
in a great brass pot
agni had arrived
and shiva some say

god is in the soles
of our dancing feet
in the palms
of hands that drum
in the eyes of the watchers of the milk
in the voice of the priest
in the heat of the fire
in the milk frothing over
out of the mouth of the vessel—

"an orgasm!" says one
"a birth!" says another[98]

After that elephant blessing the marvels began. That night Shanti and I both dreamt of rainbows. Shanti saw a double rainbow—which she understood as a blessing on her two cultures—birth and adoption. I saw a rainbow in the shape of a great U, like the U-turn this journey was in my life, returning to the place where I had begun. The next day we hired a driver to take us to Mahabalipuram. After we had seen the beautiful shore temple and thrown flowers on Vishnu still sleeping as he had been thirty years ago; after we visited the five Pandavas and seen Draupati's bedroom (she was the wife of all five brothers in the Mahabharata); after we saw the great elephants descending to the Ganges, our driver took us south of Chennai, to an unknown temple teeming with pink and blue divinities in the South Indian style. He told us to take off our shoes.

After we entered the temple a man in a blue plaid lungi, with strangely mottled skin, informed us he was our guide. He asked if Shanti was our daughter. We were surprised. People don't usually figure this out so readily. We said "yes." He asked Shanti if she was a Hindu. She said "yes." He gestured to Dan and me to stay and took Shanti into the 'Hindus Only' section of the temple. Dan and I stood there, tears in our eyes. In that psychological and spiritual elegance we met so often in India, our guide performed the ritual of initiation, separating Shanti from us, taking her into the mysterious realm of her own religious background. When she came out with red sindu on her forehead and a blessing from Parvati, Dan, in his inimitable fashion, announced she was a HinJew. Our guide, in the fashion of his country, also blessed Dan and myself, putting red sindu on our foreheads, and then hustled

---

98 Lowinsky, *red clay is talking*, p. 135 and originally in *DAYbreak*.

us for money. I will never forget the beggar girl with beautiful eyes and deformed legs. She dragged herself around on her arms and had a whine that cut into our minds. She got money out of our pockets. Always the marvelous cohabited with the terrible, the sacred with the shocking.

When we came to Ongole, the town where Shanti had been born in a missionary hospital, we learned that the hospital no longer existed, that it was a ruin. I remembered the moment I had first seen Shanti, carried Indian style by a nurse on her hip, so wide eyed, so beautiful. She was ten months old, had been born in the hospital to a mother who could not keep her. I remembered the conversation I had with my then husband, soon to be her father: "Well, why not? We've got two. A third would be fun." Neither one of us had any idea of the complexities of international adoption. This child became ours through her father's labor—luckily he knew how to work with both Indian and American bureaucracies. Now, thirty years later, I wandered around in that ruin, and tried to visualize where the nursery had been. Suddenly, a woman emerged out of the ruins. Shanti will tell you what happened next.

All of a sudden an Indian woman around 60 wearing a long pink and white nightgown/house coat appeared and . . . asked if we were looking for Clough Memorial Hospital.

Excited and surprised, we said "yes" and walked up to her. She said "I used to work at Clough Memorial Hospital from 1964-1980." So we told her I was born there in 1968. We were all so happy. She invited us into her home and told us as we entered "This used to be the maternity ward. This is where I worked . . ."

It took everything I had not to cry, but I did a little anyway. She looked teary at moments too. For her, Clough Memorial Hospital meant a lot. She took great pride in it because according to her, "It was the best hospital in South India . . ."

I sat there and felt the goodness exude from this strong, sturdy, solid, soft, maternal woman. I knew then that I had been well taken care of when I was a baby . . .

When Dan said he wanted to take a picture, she quickly ran in the other room and put on her sari. I asked if I could see the delivery room. She said of course and pulled me right in. She said there were two beds for deliveries and showed me where they had been. By now, she could understand how important it was for me to see where I was born. Her maternal/nurturing instincts took right over and she pulled me close to her body for the picture. It felt so good! She probably carried me on her hip at some point many times . . .

Esther's face and body looked like the Indian woman I had a dream about some years back—only Esther's hair had grey in it and in my dream, the lady had black hair. But, same body, same eyes, same way of standing— very grounded.

The Temple of the Complete Human Life

These were the marvels of India: elephant blessing, rainbow dreams, Shanti's initiation into the 'Hindus Only' section of the temple, the appearance of Esther, whom we liked to imagine had delivered Shanti into this world. There was another marvel for Shanti, her trip alone back to Mumbai where she felt so comfortable staying with our friends that she now feels she has family in India. Our trip to Orissa to see the great Sun temple at Konarak was another marvel, and it helped me to reorient to this time of my life, when the sun is beginning to descend.

I say to the East of me: Help me. How can I tell this story? So much I can't remember, and my notebook stolen! Shanti wasn't with us. Back home where the gods have been drained out of the sky, how can I recapture my experience in Orissa?

The goddess of many names smiles at me. You have another book that wasn't stolen. Your friend Ushah gave you a book of the poetry of Tuka, the greatest Maharastran poet of the 17th century. She told you that in Maharastran culture, 'says Tuka' is a basic expression. Tuka knows that all you need is within you. Listen:

> Words are the only
> Jewels I possess
> Words are the only
> Clothes I wear...[99]

That's lovely. But I still don't know where to begin. I feel more like that poem of Tuka's that goes:

---

99 Tukaram, *Says Tuka*, p. vi.

Where does one begin with you?
O Lord, you have no opening line.[100]

She who has many names, goddess and Muse, speaks calmly, slowly.

So you need my help. Take a deep breath. Go inward. Listen to yourself who is me. There is no difference between us. We are the same, only I take you down to the deeper layers of yourself.

It is said, when the Aryans invaded India they were already patriarchal. But the Dravidian culture they invaded, of which Shanti is a biological child, was profoundly matriarchal. There was something so fierce, so strong, so powerful in that old matriarchal consciousness that it has survived all the patriarchal layers. That is what makes you feel so deeply at home in India—you walk on female ground.

You thought the magic would be over after you left Ongole, Shanti's birth place: the magic of Esther, who had the same body build as the woman in Shanti's dream, the magic of the elephant who blessed you, and of the temple guide who initiated Shanti into Hinduism, the magic of the dreams you both had, daughter and adoptive mother, of different rainbows. Shanti is off on her own in Mumbai, putting her roots down in her native soil, and you and Dan have the last part of the journey to yourselves.

Listen to me! I speak in the manner of the poems of Bilhana, that 11th century lover turned poet, who began his poems with the phrase, "Even now," evoking the eternal present tense of poetry and of India:

> *Even now*
> *I remember her eyes*
> *trembling, closed after love*[101]

Even now, in the eternal present of memory, I see you looking through a hotel window at a huge tree and beyond it, a city full of temples sacred to Shiva. This is Bhubaneshwar, in Orissa, where the huge Lingaraj, great phallus seen all over town, is open only to Hindus. Even now, I see you standing at one of the temples. Your guide is a skinny passionate man who swings over the temple wall using his powerful arms and dragging his mostly useless legs. Dan is tired and stands outside the wall under trees, watching cows, taking photographs. Your

---

100 Tukaram, *Says Tuka*, p. 6.
101 Bhartrihari and Bilhana, *The Hermit and the Love-Thief*, p. 112.

guide is taking you around the temple, telling the stories of the gods carved into stone.

Here is Shiva, smoking marijuana. Here is Ganesha, with the elephant head. You see him at Shiva and Parvati's wedding. How can that be? Ganesha is always called the son of Shiva. But he is not. How can that be? I'll tell you how. Do you remember the story he told you? This, more or less, is how it went:

This is the temple of Shiva, lord of destruction. This is Parvati, he loves her. They are together, but this is not how Ganesha begins, though they call him Shiva's son. Parvati wants a bath. She wants to sit by herself in lotus petaled water. But she knows Shiva is amorous, would sooner have one leg around her than on the ground. So she waits until Shiva leaves to do whatever a god does on business in the Himalayas. In her bath she takes a shell from the Bay of Bengal, scraps the dirt and secretions off her body and pats them into a handsome boy. She fills him with her own breath. He is her own singular creation. And she says to him: "Guard my solitude!"

Even now, I can hear Parvati crying. Her voice is cutting the fabric of the sky as Shiva cuts the head off her son. Even now I can see Shiva's shocked face: What has he done? He only meant to love his lady. He can never resist her breasts floating in the lotus petaled water. Even now I see him wandering the jungle through the coconut palms looking, looking for some head to replace her gone son's. At last he finds that fine young elephant whose head became Ganesha's. That is why (your guide explained) Parvati's son is called the lord of obstacles. He is the only one who dares to get between Shiva and the object of his desire! This is the story you needed to hear, even now, you need to hear it again and again: what the goddess creates out of her own body, her own experience, her solitude. She has a son out of her own skin, Ganesha, the elephant headed God, a son of the mother and the animal realm. His origin is out of the deep strata of matriarchal consciousness.

Even now, I see you looking out of a car window in Orissa at what Dan is calling "green grottos," deep views through coconut palms, mango trees, neem trees, cashew trees, banyan trees, to clusters of mud thatched houses. It is the time of the rice harvest. The farmers are putting their boiled rice grain, brown in its husks, out on the road to dry. They form a golden brown runner of kernels on the side of the road. Your driver, a dignified former military policeman who tells you that everyone calls him "mama," tells you the villagers do not have enough space in their homes to dry the rice. So they do it on the road.

You see bright green rice paddies, lean dark men crouching, transplanting the rice. In the field you see a pair of bullocks linked to a plow. The farmer, head wrapped in a white turban and white lungi pulled up around his knees, follows behind. He has been ploughing the land this way for thousands of years. Everywhere there is a temple, with the bright colored Hindu dieties cascading down the steep roofs. Everywhere a shrine. Every field with cattle or crops is made sacred by the presence of a god and flowers and incense and devotees.

You are uncomfortable, sitting so long in the car. You need to relieve yourself. You are envious of Dan's easy access to the side of the road, doing as all the Indian males do. But what do the women do? Finally, in extremis, you break through what feels like a taboo and ask "Mama," that dignified man, if there is a "toilet for ladies." He says: "No—you have to go outside, but I will show you where." He stops the car at a deserted part of the road. Up a rise at some distance is a huge banyan tree. The air roots create a nest, and a dip in the ground makes for perfect privacy.

Even now, I see you entering the banyan tree nest and gasping, for you have seen my image, a black female idol, made of clay and plastered on a black board, bedecked in red clothing, with fresh yellow marigolds around my neck. Women were here just this morning, paying me homage, in the manner of their folk religion. And I have made sure to reveal myself to you in this form. I have been here for five thousand years in the banyan tree, in the women's secret living sanctuary.

The West of me is flooded with memory of that moment: the huge banyan tree, the air roots, the shock of recognition as I looked in the face of the idol. I knew you. I've always known you. Again, I have returned to that magical synchronistic time, the dream surrounds me. Walking in it, I see the manifestation of the divine. I knew you were with me. I knew my journey was not only to bring my Dravidian daughter back to her birthplace, but to meet some part of myself that had been disoriented since I left India thirty years ago.

A fire was lit in me then, as I moved from the first stage of life to the second. That fire was the beginning of a religious attitude that included the erotic, the creative, expressed in Shiva and Shakti, in lingam and yoni, in the delicious play between the realms of the gods and the humans, expressed in dance, in poetry, and carved in stone at the sun temple at Konarak.

Ramesh was the name of our guide. Even now I can hear him telling the stories of the temple. Dan was hearing one part of it, and I another. Dan heard about the architecture, and how the central column crumbled, and how, or so the legend goes, the Portuguese seamen thought the lodestone was throwing off their compasses, so they climbed the tower and threw it down, causing its collapse. He heard and saw the iron girders, used no place else in India. I heard the developmental story; Ramesh called it the "temple of the complete human life." As the temple traces the route of the sun each day, and through the seasons, it tells the story of the life stages: animal/child, human/adult, spiritual/old age. Brahma is god of new-life, the creative; Vishnu is god of mid-life, the preserver; Shiva is god of life's end, the destroyer.

The temple's central structure is in the form of a great chariot with twenty-four wheels, seven horses, and two attendant elephants. There is a great dancing hall. Its roof is gone, but on the sides you see the musicians and the dancers. It was built in a time when so many people had died in wars, in famine, and the monks were off in temples praying to the gods. They needed more people so they built this temple to the sun, to life, to the erotic, to promote life. There were dancing girls at Konarak, sacred prostitutes, called devadesis. They were the carriers of culture, of music and dance and poetry.

As recently as the 1950s there were still some devadesis in a temple in Jaipur. Konarak remembers the ancient tradition in which the erotic and sacred are one. Ramesh says: "All parts of life are shown on the temple. Here is a lady beating her huband because he has taken a lover; here is a man beating his wife because she has taken a lover; here is a lady who has just given birth, standing over a fire, it is antiseptic; here is a lady leaning in a doorway waiting for her husband; here is a prostitute in the same posture, leaning in a doorway, waiting for a customer. Here is a lady with two men; here is a man with two ladies. Here is a lion crushing an elephant who is crushing a man. Some say the lion is Hinduism, crushing the elephant of Buddhism, crushing the man who is Hinduism."

Surya, the god of the sun, deity in the inner sanctum, is no longer here. He has been taken to Delhi, to the National Museum. Here is a monk, high up on the side of the temple. Indra has sent a maiden down to bother him. She is clearly bothering him a lot. He is hugely erect. The child of their union, about to be consumated, will be named Bharata, that is, India. So India is the child of a hot and bothered monk and the sky maiden sent by Indra!

And I said to the East of me—why do you bring me to an erotic temple at this time of my life? And she of many names smiled and said:

This is your time to know bhakti. Bhakti is devotion. The bhakti tradition finds the sacred outside the temple, in the everyday experience of the ordinary person. The bhakti poets express the erotic energy between the human and the divine. Listen to Mirabai, most famous of Bhaktis, whose devotion is to Krishna, in a translation by Robert Bly:

Why Mira Can't Go Back to Her Old House

The colors of the Dark one have penetrated Mira's body; other colors washed out.
Making love with Krishna and eating little—those are my pearls and my carnelians.
Chanting—beads and the forehead streak—those are my bracelets.
That's enough feminine wiles for me. My teacher taught me this.
Approve me or disapprove me; I praise the Mountain Energy night and day.
I take the path that ecstatic human beings have taken for centuries.
I don't steal money, nor hit anyone; what will you charge me with?
I have felt the swaying of the elephant's shoulders . . .
and now you want me to climb on a jackass? Try to be serious![102]

The goddess smiled and then disappeared, like Krishna, like my lost luggage at the airport.

Grandmother Tiger

There is an Indian folk tale, attributed to Ramakrishna,[103] which I retell in a slightly changed version. It is about a tiger cub, whose mother was killed, and who was adopted by a herd of goats. The goats were kind to the little tiger, showed her how to eat, where it was safe to sleep. But the baby tiger had no idea who she really was. And so she did her best to act like a good little goat, eating blades of grass, bleating. Until one day a big old grandmother tiger approached the herd, and the goats scattered. The baby tiger bleated. And the grandmother tiger roared: "What is that pitiful noise you are making?" She picked the cub up by the scruff of the neck and took her to a pool of water. "Look, can't you see you are a tiger, like me?" And though at first the baby

---

102   Jane Hirshfield, *Women in Praise of the Sacred*, p. 139.
103   Heinrich Zimmer, *Philosophies of India*, p. 7.

tiger was frightened, and confused, she soon found her own roar, and the pleasure of being a carnivore, and her own true nature shone.

This is a story I could tell about Shanti. India is her old grandmother tiger. In that mysterious way that our fates are intertwined, it is also a story I could tell about myself, for India is also my old grandmother tiger.

There is one last Indian story I need to tell. This is the story of how poetry began. For my old grandmother tiger is my Muse and when I found this story I felt as if she'd showed me the face of my beloved, in the pool of water. It's a story about the first Indian poet, the poet of the Ramayana. In the frame story of the epic, the poet's name was Valmiki, and he was a thief who became a sage by meditating on the word "death" (mara) until it became the name of the god Rama (ma-ra ma-ra ma-ra ma ra-ma ra-ma). Valmiki is visited by the divine sage Narada, who is a messenger of the gods. Narada tells Valmiki the story of Rama, whose wife was stolen by a demon king. Valmiki is so filled with this story that he wanders along side the river Tamasa, pondering it. And as he walks he sees a pair of lovebirds singing in a tree. Suddenly the male bird falls, hit by a hunter's arrow. And, so the legend goes, the cry of the female, seeing her lover fall, filled Valmiki with the sound and rhythm of lyric poetry.

This story filled me and as I pondered its mystery, sitting on the little porch where I write poetry, long after India had disappeared, along came life of the moth.

life of the moth

in the final moments of the life of the moth
before i'd reached for the magazine
with *the god of love* on its cover
and crushed its brown flutter
i saw the sun on the bare branches
of the cottonwood tree
the shadow of the tall gray house
on the downhill evergreens
and you who had touched
my body so kindly this morning
remembering in your fingers
the shape of my breasts these

almost twenty years and the drape
of the silk scarves i wore for our love play
and the swelling of the moon
that's now gone
and the gift you gave me
early in love that red garnet
whose rich light glowed
on the pulse of my neck
stolen on our return
from ancient lands with a book of notes
and a necklace of many silver chains
that went into the hands of a stranger
who is giving it to whom
and where did the day go you wrapped me in silk
and my breasts were like
the darkened breasts of that Lakshmi at Ellora
oiled by the hungry rub of human hands
where did that notebook go
with the tree of life on its cover
the banyan tree i saw at Alura
backlit by the sun setting on the river

they were launching a god
with the head of a cobra
setting him free to drift on the water
it was the time of the harvest
and i saw the deep light in the brown of your eyes
that i saw the first time we
sat across a table and you ordered coffee
and i ordered spirits
of cherry and wine

i know i have held you off
for some time
there is that in your love
that would swallow me
and turn me into the shape of what lives
inside you

but in Bombay at the West End
with Krishna over our bed
and the rapture of the car horns and the crows
it seemed you could eat me up

and i would flow through you
like the morning rain and after sunlight
i'd turn into a great gray cloud
and sit on your horizon

and everything was fluid and always
changing and whoever has stolen my tree of life
book is having a dream of an Indian night—
the yellow orange and blue wings
of the butterfly we saw in the garden in Aurangabad
are the butterfly wings that are painted on the inside of the cup of
Indian tea I am drinking with milk—

the thief is painted on the walls
of Ajanta and the woman who watches him stealing
tells no one she is hearing the words
of the Buddha—

the soul of the moth i just killed
has flown into the mouth of the thief
on his way to becoming a poet—

he is watching the mating of cranes
the male is struck down by an arrow
in the surge of his love cry
and the wail of his mate
who has lost him forever
is the sound of his first lyric poem
flying into the darkness as sweetly

        as a soul leaves one body
           to enter the

              next[104]

---

104 Lowinsky, *red clay is talking,* p. 139.

Sappho at Midlife

The moon and then
the Pleiades
go down

The night is now
half-gone; youth
goes; I am

in bed alone
—Sappho[105]

When the Moon Casts a Woman Off

The muse is erotic. This is well known to the men who adore her. For me, her erotic nature can show up unexpectedly, as it did in India, or as it did during that powerful transition in a woman's life—menopause.

When the moon has cast a woman off, and she is running hot and cold in a confusion of purposes, body and soul fighting over the terms of their engagement, she may find herself lost, wandering about in a flat landscape, emptied of the drama of her cycles, unfamiliar to herself. When her soul, having lived in all the female places, isn't sure where she lives anymore; when her mind loses track of itself and falls through the cracks in the floor of her brain; when her spirit is short of breath, confused by the weather, by sudden surges of heat that lack any erotic purpose; and her womb that has been telling time, keeping her in tune with the sea and its tides, goes silent, keeping its secrets inside; she may find herself thrown back to what called her before her first blood flowered, as though soul, mind, spirit, need to root themselves again in her beginnings; her life needs to come full circle. For me, that circle brings me back to a reverie about my early sexual stirrings, and a fantasy about Sappho.

Sappho. Have you heard of Sappho? She lived 2600 years ago, in a time when the division between the erotic and the sacred had not yet hardened, when a young woman's education included the arts of love as well as of po-

---

105 Sappho, Barnard trans., fragment #64.

etry, dance and music. How is it she suddenly fills me with her presence, as though I've always known her; as though I can remember my time with her as a young woman on Lesbos: the temple to Aphrodite, the meadows with flowers we maidens wove into one another's hair; what we sang around the altar in the moonlight; as though Sappho was my teacher, my priestess, my wild older woman crush.

How can I claim to remember Sappho? She is a revered ancestor in my poetic lineage. But all we have of her poems are fragments, all we can gather of her life are glimpses, pottery shards, passages in Longinus and Demetrius. Yet even those fragments, those glimpses, give us a lot. They say she is a great lyric poet, perhaps the greatest of all time. They say that she, like Socrates, taught the young. The aristocrats of 5th century B.C. Greece, sent their daughters to Sappho, to her *thiasos*, where she initiated them into the mysteries of love; taught them ritual, poetry, dance, officiated at their weddings.

The Greeks did not divide sexuality up as do we. Young women learned love, their bodily and emotional responses, from other women. Some of them went on to marry men and live what we call heterosexual lives. Others stayed in the temple, as priestesses. Some, it is clear from Sappho's work, preferred to stay with women.

As Judy Grahn points out in a powerful evocation of Sappho in her book of essays, *The Highest Apple*, Sappho was born into a now lost lineage of women poets that stretched behind her for a thousand years.[106] She lived in changing times. Already by her time, Greek women were oppressed and controlled by the patriarchy; they could not own property; they belonged to their husbands. But on Lesbos, in Sappho's thiasos, we catch a glimpse of a world where, in Grahn's words "women were central to themselves." I long to have access to such wholeness of female being, such authority of voice and image.

> I took my lyre and said:
> Come now, my heavenly
> tortoise shell: become
> a speaking instrument[107]

Would I could be such a speaking instrument. Would I could summon such elegance and clarity. In Sappho female flesh becomes word. Her poems

---

106 Judy Grahn, *The Highest Apple : Sappho and the Lesbian Poetic Tradition*, p. 7.
107 Sappho, fragment #8.

are personal, embodied, full of desire and of sensuous physical detail: descriptions of beautiful clothes, advise on what flowers a girl should wear in her hair. They are luminous.

H.D. brought Sapphic lucidity back into the language, describes Sappho's poetry as: "containing fire and light and warmth, yet in its essence differing from all these, as if the brittle crescent-moon gave heat to us, or some splendid scintillating star turned warm suddenly in our hand like a jewel, sent by the beloved."[108]

I wish I could study poetry with Sappho; learn to speak from female passion as did Sappho; I wish I could be on as intimate terms with Aphrodite, know the altar, know the ritual.

> You know the place: then
>
> Leave Crete and come to us
> waiting where the grove is
> pleasantest, by precincts
>
> sacred to you; incense
> smokes on the altar, cold
>
> streams murmur through the
> apple branches, a young
>
> rose thicket shades the ground
> and quivering leaves pour
>
> down deep sleep; in meadows
> where horses have grown sleek
> among spring flowers, dill
>
> scents the air. Queen! Cyprian!
> Fill our gold cups with love
> stirred into clear nectar[109]

But wait a minute. Is this the time to be invoking Aphrodite? At midlife, dealing with hot flashes and memory loss, struggling to keep track of many obligations, is this the time of life for Sappho to be stirring in me? Sappho who loved young women, sang of their beauty, taught them the erotic mys-

---

108 H.D., *Notes on Thought and Vision* and *The Wise Sappho*, pp. 57-58.
109 Sappho, fragment #37.

teries? Where was she when I needed her, when I had never heard of her, when I was a young woman, overcome by a confusion of passions?

I came of age in a time when it was believed that young women should be sexually initiated by men. The ancient practice of a woman learning the responses of her body in the hands of an older woman, had been mostly forgotten. There was an archetype missing (still is, for the most part), one the Greeks knew well: the archetype of sacred sexuality. In my day, a young woman's passion was dangerous; if she expressed it, terrible things could happen to her. There were names: clinical names, colloquial names. Nymphomaniac. Slut. There were dangerous consequences. Pregnancies. Illegal abortions. Doors slammed for life. Shutters closed on her sense of self.

In the 1960s, some of us got wind of Sappho's energy, without really knowing much about her. We saw that women had to learn to love women instead of only valuing our relationships with men. We formed circles of women and talked personally, about sex, our bodies, our passionate lives. In such a group, "consciousness raising" we called it, I remember wondering what menopause would be like. We asked an older woman some of us knew to write a letter about her experience. I can't remember what she said. I do remember her tone, wise, funny, amazed and pleased to be asked. If I were to write such a letter now I'd have to say that nothing has prepared me for the power of change. It's archetypal, like going through puberty, or becoming a mother.

And then it occurs to me: no wonder I'm fantasizing about Sappho. It's not just that she's a priestess of Aphrodite; she's a priestess who facilitates archetypal change, and she does it in the voice of a woman-centered woman. As Judy Grahn says, when we lose access to our ceremonial stories "we fall out of history . . . out of mythic time . . . out of poetry except as the objects of it . . . out of meaning into a kind of slavery, a no-world, a no-place . . . "[110] How then can we make sense of female initiation, profound bodily changes? We need Sappho. We need her to teach us the lore of the body, the creative process, the invocation of the divine.

And I say to myself, why not try to invoke Sappho? What would it hurt? At worst she won't come. At best, we'll have an experience of the imagination.

---

110   Judy Grahn, *The Highest Apple*, p. 11.

The Tenth Muse

Imagine that we knew Sappho when we were young. Imagine that we can remember the island in the middle of the blue Aegean, near Turkey as it was 2600 years ago, a landscape of olive trees and apple orchards. The scholar of Greek lyric poetry, C.M. Bowra, describes it thus: "an abundance of natural springs fills the valleys with plane trees and lush grass; in the spring the ground is covered with anemones, orchids and wild tulips."[111] The poet Alcaeus, a contemporary of Sappho, describes her as: "violet-tressed, holy, sweetly smiling Sappho . . ."[112]

invocation

tell me, Sappho,
whose delicate fingers
wove the violets into your hair?
whose soft seashell ears burned
at your song?

and would you take her back
after the years
she forgot you

opened her body
to his song

would you come to the tip
of her tongue
leap
to her image making
mind?

would you send for her
the very chariot
that carried the goddess
she of the doves
and the smile that is

---

111 C.M. Bowra, *Greek Lyric Poetry*, p. 130.
112 Alcaeus, *Greek Lyric Poetry*, p. 239.

evening star?

lady of Lesbos
we gather
pieces of you
out of the mouths
of buried vases

i wish it were mine
to remember
how we danced
around the altar in full
moonlight
our tender young women feet
crushing the grass

holy Sappho
make a place for me now
the moon is waning
we whom the tides
have released
long for a fragment
                    of you—[113]

    She's come. Can you see her? She is so vivid, as though she's always been
here, just under the surface, energetic, curious, intense, showing off her dark
skin in bright clothing. She's wearing the purple and yellow outfit she described in a poem. Listen to her beloved Atthis:

> Sappho, if you will not get
> up and let us look at you
> I shall never love you again!
>
> Get up, unleash your suppleness,
> lift off your Chian nightdress
> and, like a lily leaning into
>
> a spring, bathe in the water.
> Cleis is bringing your best
> purple frock and the yellow
>
> tunic down from the clothes chest;

---

113 Lowinsky, unpublished poem.

you will have a cloak thrown over
you and flowers crowning your hair...[114]

She stands before a white temple, the blue Aegean glowing behind her. She's smiling at us. Sappho, speak to us!

You wonder where I've been. I say, where have you been? I've been here all along, the old voice of female poetry, glad to be released at last from all those tiresome, bookish discussions about me. You've read all that nonsense. Was I short and dark? Did I die for love? Was I married to a man called Kerkylas, a wealthy merchant, or was this an obscene pun in an Attic comedy, because Kerkylas can mean "prick from the Isle of Man"[115] Was I a love priestess? Did I have jealous fights with my rivals for love or for power? Finally you stopped reading all that scholarship that just chops me up into smaller fragments, fits me into small categories that break up my wholeness. How can you separate body from love from soul from ritual from poetry? It is only in what's left of my work that you can know me, and in the imagination of poets. There are those in your time who know me. H.D. knows me, as:

> *an island, a country, a continent, a planet, a world of emotion, differing entirely from any present day imaginable world of emotion...*
> *A song, a spirit, a white star that moves across the heaven to mark the end of a world epoch or to presage some coming glory.*
>
> *Yet she is embodied–terribly a human being, a woman, a personality as the most impersonal become when they confront their fellow beings.*[116]

Judy Grahn knows me, and traces her lesbian poetic lineage through H.D. and Emily Dickinson straight back to me.

You can know me, not only as a particular poet of 6th c. B.C. Greece, but as the fragmented voice of woman, the ghost of the wholeness of woman that's been ripped into shreds. What woman has written straight out of her body, her feeling, since I did, until now, in your time? My voice is the passion of woman for woman, the passion for the goddess. Every woman needs to know this passion, whether she sleeps with women or with men. Then she can express for herself what Freud found so mysterious: what a woman wants.

Why do you suppose you've been so consumed by poetry recently? It hasn't occurred to you that I might have had something to do with that? For two mil-

---

114 Sappho, fragment #43.
115 Sappho, *The Poems and Fragments of Sappho*, translated by Jim Powell, p. 33.
116 H.D., *The Wise Sappho*, pp. 58-59.

lenia I was a sleepy spirit. But I've been right under the surface, waiting to be invoked. I have not been forgotten, but my poems, what has become of my poems? I wrote them down. I wanted them to last forever. It looked like they would. The Alexandrians published me a few centuries after my death. My work survived for a thousand years. I was known as the tenth muse, first among lyric poets, the queen of poetry. Once, everyone knew my poetry by heart. My words were ripe fruit on the tongue of every cultivated person. Now, all that's left are fragments.

Don't think because I'm a shade, I don't mourn the loss of my work. Don't think it doesn't humiliate me, even in death, that my voice got torn to shreds of papyrus, that handwritten copies of my work were used to stuff a coffin, mummify a crocodile. Why did my books disappear? I have not been forgotten, but my poems are lost. I have not been forgotten, but for two thousand years who has written in my tradition? I have been quoted but the whole shape and luster of my work has been lost. Who has invoked me intimately, as I did Aphrodite, as you just did me? Why has it taken you so long? I've been knocking at the door of your consciousness most of your little life!

Dead poets long to be read. We long for our living audience, for the poets we influence, the poems that carry on our tradition, bring it into new territory. Suddenly your time is full of women poets, as though a fire swept through old woods releasing seeds that haven't sprouted for 2600 years! You're waking me up, exciting me, calling on me to return.

Now you want me to help you in this second rite of passage, in the Lesbos of your imagination. But I need your help. Events keep tearing you away from me. Important meetings. Conferences. Telephone calls. I say: come to Lesbos; make time for solitude; be alone with me. Imagine yourself in the grove of apple trees. The apples are reddening, growing ripe. The breeze in the trees has more to say to you than any group of colleagues. What do they know of your essence, your struggle to release your spirit from other people's purposes? If I am to help you find the self you left behind, I need your full attention, your ear to my voice, your mind to the flow of images. Most of all I need your body!

You want my body?

No, I'm not propositioning you, not in the usual sense. I'm a ghost, a spirit. What I want is words for your body's experience, your desire, your longing. When young women came to me on Lesbos I prepared them for the changing of the gods in their bodies. I called down Aphrodite. I taught them the pleasure of their bodies, what flowers to wear in their hair, what would make the blood

run hot under their soft skin. Here they were, young and so lovely, breasts just
blossoming. How could I not fall in love? I who was teaching them to cultivate
the goddess of love, to make her incarnate in their own flesh, was cultivating
my own body of love.

I brought girls from childhood to womanhood, teaching them to sing and to
dance, to cultivate the subtle play of blood and fire in their loins, the connection
to their feet, to know what colors to wear, how a dress should drape.

If I had known you when you were young, you would have known your own
beauty. You would have learned to express your own passion, in words. No
matter how overcome with passion a woman may be, if she can make a poem
of her experience—she retains herself—has made a vessel for herself. I did this
time and again.

> He is a god in my eyes
> the man who is allowed
> to sit beside you—he
> who listens intimately
> to the sweet murmur of
> your voice, the enticing
> laughter that makes my own
> heart beat fast...[117]

Can you imagine how it is to love a young woman, train her in the erotic
arts, and then have to officiate at her marriage? Making poems held me together, as making poems has been holding you together in the change of life. What
you need is some of our ancient Greek love for our bodies. We did not suffer
from that post Christian fear of the body which has caused the fragmentation of
my voice. Nor had we any desire to "rise above" our bodies. We knew what you
need to remember: the body is where the gods speak to us. Your body is speaking to you, in hot flashes, in memory lapses, in a deep disorientation from the
moon. You need me to help you in this change of the gods. I need you to give
poetic voice to the change.

There is something I don't understand. Do you not know about the
change? Didn't women of your time live past menopause?

Of course. Women have always known about menopause. In the ancient
world we had our secret rituals, we knew the herbal remedies, all the lore of the
wise blood. But none of this was valued, or written down. And as the men took

---

117 Sappho, fragment #39.

over, and women's spiritual practices were deemed dangerous, witchcraft, you forgot what we once knew. It got lost, like the poems of the poets before me, lost like the mysteries of Eleusis, like the many forms of the goddess.

What Kind of She God?

You are only now beginning to remember the power of the change of life, that it can return you to your earliest creative passion. Many of you are given more time than we were, time to shape a whole new stage of life, time to bring voice back to the woman at midlife. Maybe she sleeps alone, maybe she sleeps with a lover of many years. Maybe she has a new love. Maybe her passion is for her creative work. Does she long for the young woman she was? Does she know who she is becoming?

In the Lesbos of your imagination, I need your voice to flesh out the crossing over. I want a dialogue: my voice, your voice. I want a call and response over the millenia. Here is what's left of a poem of mine about Anactoria. She had to grow up, become a wife, leaving her youth, her beloved Atthis and me, on Lesbos. I imagine her among Lydian women, longing for us:

> Yes, Atthis, you may be sure
>
> > Even in Sardis
>
> Anactoria will think often of us
> of the life we shared here, when you seemed
> the Goddess incarnate
> to her and your singing pleased her best
>
> Now among Lydian women...
> > She wanders
>
> aimlessly . . . her heart hanging
> heavy with longing in her little breast
>
> She shouts aloud, Come! we know it.[118]

---

118 Sappho, fragment #40.

Now, how about your poem about puberty and menopause, about the fragmentation of the older woman who remembers a very different youth from that on Lesbos: your only saving grace is your grandmother's fierce eye.

Wait a moment! You know my poems?

Of course. I'm always entering poems that speak to my subject matter. Who do you think has been hanging around in you, making you feel irritable and off center until you find the right word? Understand, I'm your particular Sappho, the old female voice as it comes through you. Other poets give us other Sapphos. H.D. has her version of me. Judy Grahn has hers. There are so many of you returning my spirit to flesh, to the word.

Sappho, I feel self-conscious about my poem. What if you don't like it?

I am beyond like or dislike. I am a ghost, the spirit that enlivens your poetry. You decide what you like. I'm just hungry for your words. Your life in poetry is my continuity. It is the job of the living poet to be in conversation with the dead poets. It is the job of the dead poet to find living poets to speak through. Now don't be pussyfooting around, full of stultifying humility. You don't have time for that nonsense. Be fierce about your work. Come on, give me the poem!

Alright, alright Sappho. The poem is called:

midsummer passages at 12 and 50

that summer
child's feet jumped

        two sizes

        woman's breasts
            dragged me
            into the aching orbit of the moon

      i couldn't stand
            for looming
            over my mother

            much too big
            a girl for anyone

            to comfort
            only my grandmother's

fierce eye
could penetrate—

that summer I learned
this writing down of words until they sing
            could carry my dis–
                  membered body all the way
                        from June
                        to Labor Day—

this summer
            what's looming
                  is my end—

Four hundred and twenty moons
            have sung to me
            if I'm to be done with waxing
                  what is there left?

What kind of She God is she
                  knocking on the other side of midnight

            who ties me to the weeping willows
            by the river where we lived
            who harrows me with hot and wet lashes

                  and would detach me

                  from the moon?

This summer I am lost
            in broken languages
                  smashed spellings
                        of Her body's many names

in dreams i strike out
            at an old bat

            until I recognize her
                  penetrating eye

                        she knows
                        the darkest cavern

has the spiny wings
to carry me
back

home[119]

What kind of She God is she? That's always the first question in a ritual. Who are you worshiping? Whom do you invoke? To whom do you make your offering? For this mid-life ritual we need a new She God, no longer Aphrodite. Maybe she's different for different women. Some worship Artemis, some Demeter. Some love Athena, though you can't really take her too seriously. She thinks she has no mother, that she was born out of her father's forehead. Not good credentials for a creativity based on the female body.

This is the time for you to cultivate a ritual attitude. Take time to breathe, to gather all the pieces of yourself into the bowl of your belly. Take time to make an offering, for this puts your body in right relation to the gods, to bend to what is, offer what you value, give thanks for what you have received. Take time to call me down from the sky, up from the underworld, out of the trees and the grasses, into your tongue, your pen, your body.

Listen to me, I want to be your goddess, the She God of your immediate experience, of living ritual, the now of your breathing belly, your altered mind. I want to be sacred to you, the object of your worship. If you let me in, create a space for me, I will give you the wings of imagination, for imagination is what the gods give mortals to make up for what was taken from you when you were born. I will teach you the pleasures of creativity. In exchange, I want your offerings, your flower petals, stones, seashells, your time, your words.

Sappho, excuse me, I don't mean to be rude, but, even if you have been dead for 2600 years, you were a mortal. Isn't it presumptuous even for a spirit to want to be worshipped as a god?

Orpheus was a mortal —a priest, a poet. They turned him into a god. Why not me? That's just your Jewish–Christian thing, to make such a big demarcation between gods and mortals. But Christ became a man, and in Judaism God is equated with the breath, so you Jews are breathing God in and out of your body all the time. What a wonderful image! What you lack is a She God who loves women, who mixes the creative and the erotic. You need a She God whom

---

119 Lowinsky, originally published in *Nexus*.

you can know like a sister, a friend, a lover, a She God whom you can imagine coming to you, in the Lesbos of your imagination. Imagine my hands on your face. What is it that is written in these lines? What story do the grief marks tell? What lost love, unhappy childhood, unlived life? What habits of holding your worry, your wonder, shapes your expression? Imagine me reading your untold story with my fingertips.

It's time to know the full weight of things—weight of the belly, the breasts, the thighs. Let the full weight of your age, what you have achieved and what you haven't, who you have become and who you haven't, settle into my open palm like a falling breast, a ripe fig: full weight of your life's treasure, disappointments, bodily changes.

The maiden who is first learning about love must walk in the garden, gathering flowers; she must know herself as part of the blossoming world. She must be admired for her body's beauty, its magic. In this second initiation a woman enters another garden, a garden of herbs, of plant magic. Imagine me walking with you out into the fields to find medicinal plants: angelica, cypress, verbernum, blue cohash, motherwort. We'll look for deer antler and tortoise shell, good for slowing hot flashes. We'll walk to the sea and collect kelp and sea weed. In this time of life a woman must know herself as part of the vegetable world, born from the earth, healed by the earth, to be returned to the earth.

Feel your hot flashes, they are so interesting. What is it that insists on being known through a hot flash? That fellow you follow, Jung, quotes an alchemist who says "the stone...begins to sweat because of the narrowness of its prison."[120] I am the key to your release from that prison. Make a regular place for me. Invoke me every day, every season. Honor me and I will teach you the alchemy of words, how to find just the word that will heat up your image like a hot rock dropped into the pot. Honor me and I will teach you what men have forgotten, the alchemy of body, our luminous organ of perception; how only in body, through body, can light and spirit be transformed into being, and into the word. Let me know you, carnally, and I will give you joy of the body, words for the body, a sacred path.

Honor me and I will help you lament your losses. Any change involves loss. In my ritual for young women, I gave them poems to voice what they were losing. Here's a fragment of one, called:

---

120 *Mysterium*, CW 14 par. 34 note #227.

Bridesmaids' Carol II [121]

first *voice*	*Virginity O* *my virginity* *where will you* *go when I lose* *you?*
second *voice*	*I'm off to* *a place I shall* *never come back* *from* *Dear Bride!* *I shall never* *come back to you* *Never!*

Now, give me your poem about losing your period. It's a different kind of loss. Losing virginity is definite. You are virgin no more. But on this other side your blood disappears for a few moons, then it returns. For months, sometimes for years, you're not sure which side of the change you are on.

maybe she'll show?

maybe she'll show
and maybe she won't

my red flower
my brown stain
first seen
by my sharp–eyed mother

my ache
my shame
my descent from a cave in the earth
my place in the eyes of the moon
my delta
my tides

---

121 Sappho, fragment #32.

she has ways
strange ways
maybe she'll fill me with rust
fill me with ravings
with the rant of her fire
maybe she'll kiss me
maybe her lips
will entice me to flower
hot rose
to astonish a lover
maybe she'll drag me down
by the weight of my breasts
and bury my riot of body
down
down

below the bottom
of the sea

maybe she'll swim back to me
sweet manatee
willow that weeps

angel that strikes
singing the ten thousand things
brushing my hair
oiling my skin
slapping my face with her hand of what's real

maybe she'll never come back
my siren
my half fish
my banshee
my wanton
my slut

where has she gone?
the shadows grow longer
we are moving away from the sun

where are my mother's eyes now
and how will i know
                    the shape of my lust?[122]

---

122 Lowinsky, *red clay is talking,* p. 84.

How will you know the shape of your lust? That's a big question for your time of life, but not for young women. You just show them how their bodies work and they're off and running. When I fell in love with those young women, Hero the trackstar from Gyara[123] or little monkey faced Atthis,[124] I felt full of possibilities, theirs, mine, life, sun, flowers. Pre-nuptial rituals are all about possibility. The bride does not yet know the shape of her story. Now, at the other side of that crescent boat ride, having loved and birthed, having been sent into exile and survived it and returned, here we all are, in the Lesbos of your imagination, 26 centuries after my time, creating a temple for the change in you. You are no longer pulsing with what can happen, who or what will be born of you. Most of the story has been told, it is written into the lines of your face.

Honor me and I will teach you to become a lover to the one you were, to know your own story, to sing the song of your own lost blossoming. Out of the meeting of what is ebbing away, and what comes in anew, a new goddess is born, a new stage of life, a new quality of being. You think you have lost Aphrodite, but suddenly she is everywhere, in everything. The erotic no longer resides in your singular body, your small life with its reaching and longing. It is in everything you hear, taste, touch, smell, feel; it is in what comes to your sixth sense, of ghosts, of gods, of other realms. It is in the leaves of the tree, in your memories of who you were, in the words you find to remember yourself.

It is erotic to know your own life. It is erotic to make poems. What I have done for young women's bodies, I can do now, for your writing: teach you to follow the path of desire, to listen to what wants to be said, to stimulate what wants to be aroused.

A poem must begin in the body, like desire. You must follow the flow of voice, images, as you follow the flow of arousal in sex. And just as your lover must know exactly how to touch you, and where, the poem requires just the right touch, the right body part, the right season, flower, color, phase of the moon. If you get it right the poem begins to breath. It is its own true self, has a life of its own. And when that happens everything changes, like an orgasm. Everything moves together: flesh, muscle, mind, heart, sound, soul. Everything, flies, shimmers, cascades, cries out, falls into satisfied place.

Invoke me regularly. Make offerings to me and I will come in many forms: I'll be the voice in the back of your mind that won't shut up until you write me down; I'll be the golden eagle that flies past your window, sits on the power

---

123 Sappho, fragment #78.
124 Sappho, fragment #50.

pole, pulls you out of doors; I'll be the yellow leaf that falls to your feet, the deer and her fawn who stop you on your morning walk, she cocks her ears at you, actually steps toward you. I'll be whatever pulls you into the sensuous now, the smell of the season changing, the poem that insists on being written. I will bring you back images of the young woman you were, who and what you loved; I will help you find words to say to her. Here is a fragment of a love poem to a young woman, about what I remember:

> *If you forget me, think*
> *of our gifts to Aphrodite*
> *and all the loveliness that we shared*
>
> *all the violet tiaras,*
> *braided rosebuds, dill and*
> *crocus twined around your young neck*
>
> *myrrh poured on your head*
> *and on soft mats girls with*
> *all that they most wished for beside them*
>
> *while no voices chanted*
> *choruses without ours,*
> *no woodlot bloomed in spring with-*
>   *out song . . .*[125]

   Give us one more of your poems because it demonstrates something that keeps amazing you, and still amazes me after 2600 years: the alchemy of poetry. Something tugs at you, a phrase, an image. It has life energy, and if you honor it, if you follow it, you can unlock what you didn't know you had locked away, you can discover what you never knew you knew: you work on the poem and the poem works on you. You hear a phrase, for example—"when Aphrodite danced in me" and it comes back again and again until you go with it, and suddenly you have a clear image of the young woman you were, an image you haven't remembered for years. Then a dream image leaps in, stirs up the brew and you're transformed into a lover you never had! You feel it—physiologically, psychologically. The poem is the alchemist and you are the work. Let's hear what happened to that phrase, "when Aphrodite danced in me."

---

125 Sappho, fragment #42.

when aphrodite danced in me

i thought she was me
that the crash and the moan
    and the ebb were my own—
           gold coin
              from under the sea—
              sun drenched
                    abandon—
    my breasts have fallen

        i've lost my shoes
        if i could only see

the one i used to be
i'd sit her on this rock
        on the beach

        in that burnt orange minidress
                remember?

                i wore at 33?

unbind her breasts
release her hair
admire her long lean legs

i'd be her raunchy old goat
        of a painter lover
        ask her to dance for me
           one more time
        at the edge of the world

        drum beats
        She who comes out of the foam
           has made me a silver
           casket of words

              to hold this
                loss[126]

You see, by being open to a phrase that won't let you go, you've evoked me. Know that I long for you, as you have longed for me. I long for your deep attention—to find the exact word, the precise image. I long to be brought back into

---

126 Lowinsky, unpublished poem.

language, into your everyday experience of the sacred breathing world. I am that spirit that is known only in the flesh. I am the ancient human soul; you almost lost me. I'm always cruising the three realms looking for whose body can give me a voice. Make a regular place for me in your life. Light me aflame. Do not forget me. Do not forget me . . .

Helena is a Root Vegetable

Myth is the story told of what cannot be told, as mystery is the scene revealed of what cannot be revealed . . . This is not a story of what he thinks or wishes life to be, it is the story that <u>comes to him</u> and forces his telling. Wherever life is true to what mythologically we know life to be, it becomes full of awe, awe-full. All the events, things and beings of our life move then with the intent of a story revealing itself.

—Robert Duncan[127]

Dionysus Came from Thrace

The word mystery comes from the Greek, to close the eyes, to close the lips, or from muein, to initiate. Mystery is what appears to us when we close our eyes and look into our own darkness—the place where gods and humans meet. The word myth means to make the sound *mm*—to mutter or to mumble, to be inarticulate. We are filled with something unutterable, and we seek a way to utter it. In the tension between what is so much bigger than we, and what we can translate into language, the Muse enters. She may rip you apart or fill you with ecstasy. Or are they the same thing? For a moment she gives you a way to hold her power. Then, she is gone.

Yet fragments are of the essence of creativity. And fragments are what lead me. They tug at my psyche, opening doors, taking me into new realms where maybe a poem will begin, or a journey. A phrase from a myth, "Dionysus came from Thrace," tugs at me for years. In a dream a horse in the shape of the famous one in the cave painting at Lascaux, runs toward me out of the paleolithic and ends up in a poem. An image in a magazine, an ancient golden libation bowl, a three dimensional mandala with an omphalos in the center demands my attention. The article tells me this beautiful sacred object was looted from a grave, and now decorates the grand piano of a hedge fund manager in Manhattan. I can neither explain the numinosity of the image, or the rage I feel at its theft, until it finds its way into a poem and calls itself the "golden navel of the world." When it works, poetry can gather the numinous fragments that take me over, that seem to possess me, into a satisfying pattern. But often, for days, sometimes weeks, I can't find the thread to gather

127 Robert Duncan, *Fictive Certainties*, p. 2.

these fragments. When I do, it is an indescribable high. This doesn't only happen in poetry. It can happen on a journey. It happened in Bulgaria.

What mystery is it that shapes ordinary events into the stuff of our most numinous meanings? What mystery was it that took me to Bulgaria, there to show me so many faces of my Muse? On one level it was the mystery of marriage. I am married to an extrovert who loves traveling the world and wants, whenever possible, for me to join him. I like to travel too, but my nature is on the introverted side, and I am pulled to mystical experience. My husband, Dan, had consulted for a number of years to non-governmental organizations in the Balkans. He kept telling me that I had to come to Bulgaria, I would love it. I wasn't exactly sure why.

"So," Dan said to me, as we approached our 20ᵗʰ year of marriage, "how about a trip to Bulgaria to celebrate our anniversary?" "Bulgaria?" I asked. I'd been thinking Hawaii. Maybe Italy. "Why Bulgaria?" "You'll love it" he said. "I just know it." He hadn't won me over, not yet.

Dan knew of my fascination with the myth of Dionysus. He knew that the simple phrase with which many versions of the myth begin: "Dionysus came from Thrace" had, for unknown reasons, always sent a chill up my spine. He knew that I was always on the look-out for Thrace. Thrace. Where was Thrace? It held some sort of numinous resonance for me. What did it mean that Dionysus came from somewhere else? Once, in Ohrid, Macedonia, on a trip I'd made to join Dan, I found an astounding brass sculpture in a dusty little museum. A small, perfectly formed, naked dancing maenad, with a snake wrapped around her. I could find out very little about her, except that she was probably made in the 4ᵗʰ c. B.C. Maybe, I thought, this was Thrace. But the Macedonians shook their heads. They were Macedonians, not Thracians!

One day, alone with my writing, I got a call from Dan, who was traveling again. "Guess where I am?" he asked. "Bulgaria, I think." "Yes, but where?" "Sofia?" "No," he said "I'm on the plain of Thrace!" A chill ran up my spine—I had to go.

And, as happens when one is following a charged path, things began to happen. At the time the San Francisco Jung Institute was hosting an international scholar, Tedy Petrova, who comes from Bulgaria. Dan and I had dinner with her. When I mentioned Thrace her eyes lit up. She had studied Thracian culture and mythology. Yes, of course, Dionysus came from Thrace. This was not news to her. Didn't we know, Thrace was the ancient name of the land now known as Bulgaria? Again that movement of energy along my spine, kundalini stirrings, what was awakening? What was pulling me?

Tedy connected me with her mentor, Krassimira Baychinska. Krassy and I began e-mailing. Krassy wrote me that the site of Dionysian cult practices was in the Rhodope mountains, which were very beautiful. She and her husband knew them well. Were we walkers? They would be happy to show us this area. The mountains were not steep, she said, they were soft and feminine, and easy to walk in. Krassy invited me to give a lecture and a workshop in Sofia. I sent her "How Eurydice Tells It," on the underworld aspects of the Muse whose visitation I've described earlier. I did not know until Krassy informed me, that Thrace was not only the home of Dionysus, but of Orpheus and Eurydice!

There is another glowing fragment that clung to me during this time. It was a dream I had before going to the Balkans for the first time (that was the trip to Macedonia I mentioned, in which I met the little dancing Maenad). It was a simple dream. A voice said: "Helena is a root vegetable." And I saw an image of a root vegetable, a potato or a parsnip, all dressed up in a gauzy summer frock. For reasons I could not understand, this was enormously numinous.

I began to get what the dream was about in the museum at Skopje, the capital of Macedonia. I saw a clay figure of a bird headed goddess, very primitive, very ancient, like the ones dug up by the archeologist Marija Gimbutas. "Oh," I said "there's Helena!" I got it again in somewhat different form, when, on a mountain trail, Dan and I saw a group of old women wearing babushkas, coming down the mountain. Their faces looked like root vegetables. Their pockets were full of herbs and roots that they had dug up. "Oh," I said again, "there's Helena!"

And, years later, I found in a book by Mircea Eliade a description of the cult of the Mandragora, or mandrake root. He describes how in certain regions of Romania, the women still practice an ancient magical ritual in the spring, a spell for love, for marriage. An old wise woman goes into the woods accompanied by two young girls. They go early, so that they are near the mandragora at sunrise. The wise woman finds the plant and pronounces magical formulas over it, "while the young women eat, drink spirits, talk to each other amorously, embrace, and cover each other with kisses."[128] The root is dug up

---

128 Mircea Eliade, *Zalmoxis*, p. 20.

carefully, so as not to break any part of it. In the hole they put bread, salt, and a coin, the price of the mandragora. Sometimes the women dance naked around the root. Sometimes they sew it into their clothing. The mandragora is called Wolf Cherry, Lady of the Forest, Great Lady, Empress of Herbs. "Ah," I say again, "there's Helena!"

The Root Matter

But, I am getting ahead of my story, pulled as I tend to be, by numinous fragments. Let me return to Bulgaria. It is the end of September, 1999, and I have just arrived in Sofia. Dan has been in the Balkans working for several weeks and I am reeling with jet lag. Sofia is a city of faded beauty, of old European elegance and tired good looks. Our lovely hotel looks out on a 14th century church with a verdi-gris dome, Sveta Nedalya. Behind the hotel is another much older church, built on the ruins of a pagan temple. It is Saturday. The brides are out all over town. One is standing, glowing in her white finery, on the steps of Sveta Nedalya. A feeling of something gathering is within me. Dan tells me a dream of a cheetah, a great wild cat who likes him. We walk to the huge Alexander Nevsky cathedral and I light a candle. My jet lag begins to ease.

That evening we are invited to dinner by Krassy and her husband Dincho. It is stark outside their building, that uninspired communist architecture. But inside their apartment is warm, full of books and rugs, a comfortable interior space. It strikes me that it must be emblematic of how life was here until very recently. Communism fell just ten years earlier. And because of the external controls, the paranoia, the richness of life was all interior, with friends and family. Since "the changes" people enjoy their freedom to say what they want, but struggle with economic insecurity. Luckily Krassy and Dincho were able to buy their apartment. We sit on a small balcony and begin a conversation that will last for the next seven days.

Krassy is red haired, grey eyed, intense. She tells me that she and Dincho met at the University of Moscow in the 60s. They were drawn to each other by their mutual love of the Rhodope mountains. He was studying mathematics, and she psychology. Someone in her group had access to a volume of Jung's work. She remembers that she had to sign up in advance to be able to borrow the book for one night. It was Jung's *Symbols of Transformation*. She'd never read anything like it before. Everything fell into place. She felt she had come home.

In his second edition foreword to *Symbols of Transformation* Jung writes: "I simply had to know what unconscious or preconscious myth was forming me, from what rhizome I sprang . . . For the root matter is the mother of all things."[129] Ah, Helena, again!

I tell them my father's people come from Russia, from the city of Odessa. Dincho says, "Odessa is the mother of all cities, the source of Jewish Eastern European culture." He began naming all the famous violinists who came from Odessa, sounding exactly like my father and his eternal game of Jewish one-up-manship. But Dincho is not Jewish.

Odessa is just on the other side of the Black Sea, Dincho tells us. We really should go. I feel haunted by memories of my father talking about the Black Sea. It had such a powerful ring, Black Sea. As a child I imagined it as literally black. I saw my father walking in dark woods beside it.

We spend Sunday with Krassy and Dincho in Sofia, at the museum, where Helena appears again, in her bird goddess manifestation, from the 5th millenium B.C. There is an entire room devoted to the beautiful Glagolithic alphabet, that briefly co-existed with the Cyrillic alphabet invented by the brothers Cyril and Methodius in the 9th century. Written language came late to the Thracians.

When standing in the beautiful ikon collection of the Alexander Nevsky Cathedral, I ask Krassy if she was raised in the Eastern Orthodox tradition. She gives me a puzzled look and says, "No, aethiest!" It takes me a moment to remember that the church was forbidden, that god was an opiate. But, she says, her grandmother was eastern orthodox as a child, before communism. And her mother, has recently begun going to church. How hard it is for me to imagine life without a spiritual orientation.

Monday is the day we leave for the Rhodope Mountains. Dan has rented an Audi, it handles well he says. He does all the driving. Luckily, he enjoys it. We enter the mountains, guarded by the Bachoven monastery. Dark inside, Christ is at the top of the dome, his bearded face in governing mode. An ikon of the Madonna, shows us her dark face ringed with silver, her baby's sweet silver body in her hands. Young women are on their knees, scraping up

---

129 *Symbols of Transformation*, CW Vol. 5, pp. xxiv-xxv.

candle wax. Outside, in the courtyard, there are old women around a huge cauldron, boiling down the dried peppers to make ajvar, the aromatic bright red pepper puree typical of Bulgaria and the former Yugoslavia. Next stop, Dincho says, is the "wonderful bridges." Getting there involves driving over gravel and stones. This is nothing compared to what is to come. But the stone "bridges," natural arches crossing the river, are wonderful, great round feminine forms, an opening between stone thighs, the murmur of water telling secrets of the mountains.

We drive deeper into the mountains. Red roofed houses, shepherds, farmers. This, Dincho told us, is potato growing country. Root vegetables! Helena again. We arrive at a steep village of stone houses and red roofs, tucked into the Rhodope Mountains, called Momchilovtsi. Our inn, called Shipkita, or Wild Rose Hips, is perched on a hill, looking down into the village and the valley. From our balcony, I watch an old woman in black with a walking stick making her way down the narrow street as light leaves the landscape. Our host, a big man with a broad face and smile, greets us in the dining room with the huge fireplace. He talks in rapid Bulgarian with Krassy and Dincho. They translate for us that he is telling local legends of golden treasures found in the mountains. Later I learn that many ancient treasures have been discovered in Bulgaria, made of Thracian gold. Some are part of an exhibit that was recently seen in San Francisco, of golden cups and libation bowls with intricate mythological designs. The archetypal mandala pulls at me, here it is again, the golden navel of the world that landed in my poem.

Dincho tells us that we will never taste potatoes as good as the ones that grow in the Rhodope Mountains. The best way to prepare them is to roast them directly in the embers of the fire. Our host does so. They are good, sweet tasting. Helena again!

In Mythic Time

Tuesday. This is the day we are to hike into the Rhodope Mountains. When is it that we enter mythic time? When we walk into the meadow, past a lake, into a pine forest? When Dincho, clearly a mountain man, picks up the pace with his even gait rapidly covering the ground, Dan pushing to keep up with him? Is it when Krassy, who has slightly injured her ankle and has it wrapped up in a bandage, stops suddenly on the path, her grey eyes glowing, her hands gesturing, speaking of the son of the mother and the son of the son? What is it about these phrases that sends the Kundalini snake slithering up my spine? Responding to my interest in Dionysus and Thrace she has done much reading. The mother she says, is the goddess. Her name is Cotyttia, or Bendis. She is self-fertilizing. She gives birth to the son, who is Dionysus, the son of the mother. She waits for him to grow up and couples with him and gives birth again, this time to Orpheus, the son of the son.

She talks a complex numerology: the mother is the four, the son of the mother is three, the son of the son is three. Thracian mysteries are full of number symbolism. I don't understand it. But I find it moving, magical. Is it Krassy's enthusiasm, her magical incantations that send me into the altered space that I usually visit alone, when writing? Is it that she reminds me, in some mysterious way, of a girlhood friend I've lost touch with, who had red hair, and a passionate manner? Has Krassy turned into my Muse? Or is it the view we get when we arrive at the first 'hut', actually a stone house at Prespa? This is a place where hikers can spend the night. From it we can see miles of softly rolling blue mountains. "This is all Thrace," Dincho gestures. "And over there is Greece." I look at Dan. He is transported. All four of us are in a trance.

It's just two hours to the next hut, says Dincho, and then we'll climb the first Dionysus peak. Back on the trail, Krassy is telling me about Zalmoxis, another Thracian god, who is both chthonic and solar. My way of understanding is shifting. I have seen Dionysus as chthonic, and Orpheus as his solar opposite. But in the Thracian system, as I begin to understand it through Krassy, Dionysus and Orpheus are both chthonic and solar, father and son, brothers, born directly from the Great Mother herself. Dionysus in his Zagreus form is the horned snake. He is also the divine child who has wonderful playthings and likes to look at himself in a mirror. He gets torn up by Titans. In my favorite version, Thracian, Apollo saves his heart, gives it to Semele to swallow, and she gives birth to him a second time. The name Semele comes from an Indo-European word root that means earth. She is the earth mother.

Orpheus of course has a similar fate, he is also torn to pieces. In Thracian myth he is not only a sun worshipper. He has both chthonic and solar aspects. Maybe, being torn into pieces is simply what happens when you move from darkness into light, from mythic into what we call ordinary time. Krassy and

I talk about fragmentation as the basic initiation experience of the shaman. Dionysus and Orpheus are both shamanic figures. Later I will remember what Eliade writes: "The shaman is above all an ecstatic." I will remember that the poet and the shaman were, in the beginning of culture, the same. I will remember that the horse was sacred to the shaman, the method of transport from one realm to another.

By now the men are way ahead of us on the trail. They whistle and yell for us to catch up. Reality hits Dan sooner than it does me. He is looking at his watch. It's two in the afternoon. We have been walking three hours. We are getting tired and achy. There is no way we can get to the Dionysus peak and walk back out before dark. Ever since Dan broke his leg a few years ago, he, who was once so sure footed, has a tendency to lurch. And in the dark he loses his balance. A twenty mile hike is nothing for Dincho, who spends most of his weekends walking in the mountains. But Dan and I think we've taken a serious hike when we walk six miles. And we've already walked close to nine miles. It becomes apparent that there is no way we can make it to the Dionysus peak. I am sorely disappointed. I've come all this way. But how do I know this is what I have come for? It's entirely Dincho's idea to climb to the Dionysus peak. I say, trying to be philosophical, "Life is less about peaks and more about the walk in the woods." Dincho says, "There is a spring just up ahead. We can have lunch."

There, in a green glade, next to a huge ant hill, is a bench, and a stone spring commemorating someone's dead husband and father. This is how people in the Rhodopes commemorate their dead. The mountain springs are sacred. Earlier on the trail we saw a lovely stone structure built to house a spring. There was a spigot, and a ladle for all who wandered by to drink from. On the stone was a photo of a good looking young man, and these words:

> Oh my son
> you rose too quickly
> and when you fell
>   the sun set.
>
> He was 21.

I sit on a rock by this deep forest spring, close my eyes, and let the forest speak. I see moving greenery behind my eyelids, everything is green and in motion. But it isn't Dionysus who appears to me in that glade in Thrace. It is someone very different. What mystery is this? I see a creature, Pan-like, with goat feet and human torso. It shape-shifts into a centaur whose body is covered with grape vines and leaves. He has a human face of enormous kindness, and his voice is warm. He says:

Everything is alive. Even the stone you sit on. Even the dead leaves. Even the dead are alive in me. There is no death. Climb on my back. I will carry you. I am the secret of what green does in the darkness, of what rain does, and the wind.

I feel an enormous sense of relief, of joy and of peace after this visitation. But for a long time I speak of him to no one. It feels a mystery that must be held in silence. And I am puzzled. If he had been a horse, the steed of my imagination as a young girl, I would have understood him. But a centaur? I've had no commerce with centaurs since myths have begun their pull on me. Later, with Krassy's help, I will find some articles and books on Thracian myth, and archeology. In one, called the "Rogozen Treasure," by Ivan Marazov, a famous Bulgarian archeologist, with whom we will spend a fascinating evening, and who turns out to be an old friend of Marija Gimbutas, and familiar with Jung, I find the image of winged centaurs on a 4th century B.C. jug.

Centaurs, it turns out, are an ancient tribe called the Kentauri, famous for wild, anti-social behavior. Marazov describes centaurs as representing uninitiated male energy: they live collectively on the margins of culture, do not know how to hold their liquor, violate the rules of hospitality, eat raw meat, and do not recognize the norms of marriage. They are liminal beings, who live on the boundary between wildness and culture. However, the great exception to the bestial conduct of the tribe of centaurs is Cheiron, who is not only married, but a great teacher of healing, and the tutor of Aesclapius, famous for his dream temple.

Graves mentions Cheiron often in *The White Goddess*:

> . . . the most famous school was kept by Cheiron the Centaur . . . Among his pupils were Achilles the Myrmidon, son of Thetis the Sea-goddess, Jason the Argonaut, Hercules, and all the other most distinguished heroes of the generation before the Trojan War. He was renowned for his skill in hunting, medicine, gymnastics and divination.[130]

So, it dawns on me, it is Cheiron who spoke to me in the green glade, Cheiron who is my spiritual ancestor as a Jungian, for Cheiron is the arche-

---

130 Graves, *The White Goddess*, p. 239.

type of the wounded healer and sacred to my discipline of analysis. Certainly, he is an unexpected form of my muse. His geneology is variously told. In one version he is the son of Cronos and Philyra, a nymph. Cronos, to hide his passion for Philyra from his wife, Rhea, takes on the form of a stallion. Thus Philyra gives birth to a creature who is half man, half horse. She is horrified when she sees her son and asks to be changed into anything but what she is. She is transformed into a linden tree and Cheiron is abandoned. Apollo finds him and fosters him.

Others say Cheiron is descended from Ixion, who begat the race of centaurs on Nephele, a cloud. Cheiron is accidentally wounded by his friend, Herakles, who is fighting the wild centaurs in a cave. Cheiron is in so much pain he cannot bear his immortality. He wants to die. In a complex exchange that involves Prometheus, he gives up his immortality, and Prometheus, who has been chained to a rock where a bird eats his liver, as a punishment for his disrespect for the gods, is freed. The suffering of both comes to an end.

Cheiron dies. Yet it is he who says to me, "there is no death." I have the intuition that he is telling me the essence of the Thracian mystery. Later, I will find a reference in Joseph Henderson's book *Thresholds of Initiation* to "the old Paleolithic assumption that nothing ever really dies but only transmutes its ontological state."[131] And in a book by the distinguished archeologist and Thracologist Alexander Fol, I'll read: "The mystery of Thracian Orphic religion . . . consists in the mysterious faith in immortality."[132]

The Fairy Demon, Svetkaritsa

Wednesday. At breakfast—a wonderful meal of dense yogurt, freshly churned butter, freshly baked bread, home made jams and eggs—Dincho announces: "Today we go to the second Dionysus peak. After that we will go to the cave."

Dan and I don't understand about this cave. Why is it so important? Dan expresses his desire to go to a village. There is one on our way, with a music school which teaches the mysterious Bulgarian style of singing. Our plans are changed to include the village today, on our way to the Dionysus peak.

---

131   Joseph Henderson, *Thresholds of Initiation*, p. 141.
132   Alexander Fol, *The Thracian Dionysius*, Book Two, pp. 360-361.

Tomorrow there will be time for the cave. Will we have to walk all the way up to the peak, we wonder, remembering yesterday. "I think," Krassy says, "that there is a road up."

So it is that we stop at the lovely village of Shiroka Luka, which means white forest. We take photos of each other on an arched bridge, admire the intricate architecture and the flower boxes on the houses, and wander into the music school. In the entry way we hear music. A group of young women in black leather jackets and high clunky heeled shoes, are singing in that wide-throated Rhodopian way, holding hands, having great fun. Dan is in heaven.

Our approach to the second Dionysus peak begins from a village called Zmeitza. "Zmeit," Krassy explained, "means snake." "Za" is the feminine ending. Zmeitza also has the meaning of dragon. A wild rush of kundalini climbs up my spine. In Zmeitza, which is a poor Muslim village, the dirt road is already a challenge, rutted, full of rocks. We stop to ask some young men, playing chess on a stoop, what the road up the mountain is like. They peer under the car to see how high it is. "Not bad," they say, "just be careful." Later, we wonder, could they have been serious?

A few hundred yards later we are blocked by a man moving his potatoes on a wheelbarrow in the road before us. A rickety old red car blocks what road there is. The potato farmer asks Dincho to give him a hand to push his car out of the way. We drive on, the Audi rocking over ruts and rocks, and begin to realize that we are driving more slowly than we could walk. It is early afternoon. We don't have time to walk to the Dionysus peak and back before dark. I don't think I can stand being disappointed again.

At this point Dincho has the brilliant idea of asking the potato farmer, whose car is now running and who has driven up behind us, to take us up to the peak. I wonder whether his car, which, Dincho tells us, is an old Moskovitch, a Soviet era car, probably from the 1960s, can make it to the peak.

That is how it happens that the four of us climb into Boyko Pecklivanov's potato hauling vehicle, Dincho in front, Dan, Krassy and me holding on for dear life in back. The road is terrible. Steep. Full of great ruts, holes, rocks. But this potato farmer is a cowboy. He knows just when to twist the steering wheel so the car virtually flies over the ruts. It leaps, stops, coughs, starts again. We laugh with fright and delight. "Our Pegasus!" cries Krassy. And I see again the centaur who spoke to me yesterday in the green glade and said: "Just climb on my back!"

Near the top we see a big truck with potato harvesters, women in babush-kas, men in dark cloths, bent over the brown fields. How did they get up here? Turns out there is a better road from a distant village. "But we," says Krassy, "needed to approach the peak from 'Snake.'" And, I think to myself, I needed to ride the centaur. We give Boyko Pecklivanov some money. He accepts it but makes it clear that he didn't do this for money. He tells us that the way down on foot won't take us very long. As we walk past the potato harvesters they invite us to join them for lunch. We thank them, but we want to get to the peak.

We walk through steep slopes of yellowing ferns, some still green, some turning brown, and into prickly fields of silver gray sage. "The first wall" says Dincho, pointing to a depression in the earth. I begin to feel the genius of the place, ecstatic, magical. Krassy tells me that 9 years ago, when she and Dincho first came here, and she knew nothing of Thracian mysteries, she had a mystical experience. "It was entirely unexpected," she explained. Her eyes open, suddenly she saw herself as the priest of an ancient cult, arms up at the top of the mountain, greeting the sun. Then she saw herself doing something with fire in a vessel. At the last of four walls, near the top, Dincho showed me the place where the cooking vessel was placed. We find much broken crock-ery. "Fire in a clay pot," Krassy says, "lit by oil." Later she will show me the book by Alexander Fol, who writes:

> These mountains were the inaccessible centres of the Thracian Dionysian religion and the main sanctuary of this deity must be hidden somewhere in them. In the centre of the round temple the priests prophesied by the blazing fire, contemplating in turn the sky in daytime and at night, i.e. the terrestrial and solar face of Dionysus, through the open dome of the temple.[133]

The peak, she tells us, is called Videnitza, "from where you can see a lot." And indeed, we can see the lovely Rhodope Mountains rolling away from us in all four directions. She and I both go off and sit, alone, for a few minutes, while the men hunt for pottery shards. I remember Kerenyi writing that the mystery "begins for the mystes when . . . (she) closes her eyes, falls back as it were into (her) own darkness."[134] (I have changed the gender designations).

If Krassy had another mystical experience that afternoon on the moun-taintop, she didn't tell me of it. And I didn't tell her of the maenad who ap-peared to me dancing in white drapery. The maenad, for that is who I think

133 Fol, *The Thracian Dionysius*, Book Two, p. 363.
134 Kerenyi, *Mysteries of the Kabeiroi* in *The Mysteries*, p. 39.

she is, says: "I have always been here, just behind your eyelids. I am billowing white light, I am lightning, the light in your eyes, the light of your cells, the light that is always in you. You never lose me, just close your eyes. Here at the top of the world where I dance with the ancient ones, dance among mountains, in the four directions, dance with the ferns that grow yellow and bronze in the fall, dance in the fire pot. I am light. I am heat."

Later, in Sofia, Dan will hear the story of a fairy demon, from his Bulgarian friend Anna, and he will tell it to me: how she dances in white and enchants the shepherd. If he falls asleep she will tear him to shreds. If she falls asleep he can marry her. And after she bears him a child she will leave him, and bathe herself in a mountain lake, and emerge, virgin again. Her name is Svetkaritsa. "Dan," I will say, for I have not yet spoken of my experience to anyone, the hair on the back of my neck is standing up, "I saw her, on the mountain top, at Videnitza!"

The potato farmer was right. It is an easy descent, down the mountain side. Approaching our car, we are suddenly surrounded by a herd of cattle returning to the farm in the evening, a huge black bull among them. Dionysus! At dusk we drive through an amazing canyon. The leaves are beginning to turn. We stop at the hut at Trigad to call the keeper of the house where Krassy and Dincho have arranged for us to stay. There are few official inns in the Rhodopes, mostly people arrange with locals to rent a room in their house. He showed up, a fine looking young Muslim man named Venci, driving a red car of more recent vintage than that of the potato farmer. We followed him up a rutted unpaved road.

Venci has made his big house with his own hands. We stay in the family's rooms. Their belongings are in the closet. His intense wife, Nadia, makes dinner for us. Dan has trout. I have a wonderful mix of rice, eggs, ham, onions and peppers. Outside, lightning flashes. I think of the maenad who spoke to me at the top of Videnitza, of fire and of lightning. Venci tends the fire in the huge stone fireplace, and drinks rakija with us. Nadia comes and sits, eats a little Shopska (chopped salad with tomatoes and feta cheese), drinks rakija, smokes, watches us eat. Venci's father, a gaunt man in a ripped sweater, with deep set eyes and bronze skin, comes by to see the Americans. He sits with us, drinks rakija, smokes, talks in Bulgarian to Krassy and Dincho. We learn he is talking about going over to Greece to visit his dead wife's family. Since the "changes" the boundary has become quite permeable, especially for the locals. We have come to Trigad, we learn, to go to the cave. Tomorrow,

Thursday, we will go early to the cave, before driving back, via the old town of Plovdiv, to Sofia.

The Cave of Orpheus

Thursday. After my first experience with sheep's yogurt at breakfast—very firm, salty, delicious, and eaten under Nadia's curious eye—we take our belongings out to the car and drive to a nearby cave. The storm is over. It is a clear, crisp day. At the cave, no cave keeper. Krassy says she knows where to find him. She is sure he is back in Trigad, in the bar, drinking rakija. Dincho stays at the cave and the three of us drive back to the village. Krassy is right. There he is, with the other village men, drinking at nine in the morning. She yells at him: "These people have come from America to see the cave! And here you are drinking rakija!" "No problem" he says, "I'll be right there." And so he is, zooming up on his motorscooter, opening his little shop, and the door to the great cave.

The name of the cave is Diavolskoto Garlo, which means "devil's throat cave." The British "Know How Fund" has given money to build a staircase into the cave. Upon entering, we notice a charming sculpture of a devil and I ask, "Who carved this?" "I did," answered the cave keeper. I am surprised, not expecting to be impressed with this cave keeper. Turns out he is not only an artist, but a mythologist, very knowledgeable about Thracian myth.

The cave is enormous, dark—the womb of the earth. We hold onto the long cold handrail. By dim flickerings of light we see the dark shadows of bats flying about. Down we go, down down. At the bottom, by the light of a candle, we see a charming carving of Orpheus, with a lyre. "Who carved this?" I ask. "I did," answers Kostadin, the cave keeper. "It is an altar to Orpheus. People have left money for him, and made wishes," Kostadin explains. I marvel at this. "Oh," says Kostadin, "didn't you know? This is the cave of Orpheus. Where he came to get his Eurydice out of the underworld!"

"Do you know the myth of Orpheus?" Dincho asks. "His wife, Eurydice dies. He has to come down to the underworld to get her back." "Dincho," says Krassy, "Naomi is giving a lecture about that myth tomorrow." But I don't feel offended. I feel embarrassed. Why hadn't I understood Dincho's insistence that we visit the cave? All life begins in a cave. It is womb, tomb, first human habitation. Of course we need to be here, to feel the darkness, the clamminess, the cold of the rock, the bats flying above. Kostadin the cavekeeper shows us the devil's shadow, in the deepest recesses of the cave, near a waterfall: there is indeed a shadow, with horns.

It is fearful going down into this darkness, even with the staircase and handrails provided by the British Know How Fund, even with the candles, and the subtle carvings. Cold cuts through to the bone. Darkness takes over the mind, the body, the heart. It is easy to stumble. I know myself as Orpheus. I know myself as Eurydice.

At last we begin our ascent. Climbing back up the long long staircase, holding onto the cold handrail, light creeps through a crevice. Tree roots are clutching a rock. Coming closer and closer, we finally pass through the narrow rock canal, reborn into the light. The mud of the mother is on my lavendar pants. The light is dazzling, disorienting, dismembering. I remember that Helena means light, root vegetable pushing her green head out into the light.

Later I was to read Joseph Henderson's comment that the cave was the place "where significant initiations of the shamanic type were originally performed." He dates them back to the Paleolithic. The cave keeper has told us that there are neolithic remains in some nearby caves. I would read that the cave was tomb, temple and healing shrine.[135] I would remember that Cheiron lived in a cave, and that the mysteries of Cotyttia are initiation mysteries. They involve a plunge into darkness, a rebirth through the cave.

So all that had been gathered seems to fall into place. My heart has been swallowed into Semele's womb. I've been one in the darkness with Eurydice, whose name means wide ruler, one in the darkness with Orpheus, god of poetry. I have exploded into many joyous pieces like Dionysus, god of green things, growing into sunlight.

We drive back through beautiful country, watching the leaves turn, leaving the mountains. We stop in the lovely old town of Plovdiv, for lunch in an outdoor courtyard with grape arbors. Driving back to Sofia at dusk, filled with my experiences, I find myself wondering if Dincho, walking through the Rhodopes most weekends as he does, has absorbed the ancient cult practices through the soles of his feet. I am overwhelmed by the elegance and archetypal truth of his plan for us, an initiation mystery. We entered the mountains

---

135 Henderson, *Thresholds of Initiation*, p. 141.

by stopping at the church of the latest religion, the Bachoven monastery. Then he took us to the ancient gods of stone, the wonderful bridges. Fol says that Sabazios, an ancient name for Dionysus, is a stone god. Next we are brought to the Dionysus peak, the solar aspect of the god. My spirit dances on the mountain peak. Then we are taken to the cave of Orpheus, the chthonic aspect of the god. My heart is swallowed by the earth goddess. Alexander Fol writes "Mystery is a ritual performance enacted by personified or identified cosmic principles."[136] According to this definition, had we not participated in a mystery?

Where the Old Gods Speak

Dionysus comes from Thrace, because here, where written language came so much later than it did to Greece, there was more direct access to wildness, to the raw experience of divinity. Dionysus comes from a place where magic still lives, where the dark of the cave is powerful, where Helena has not forgotten her root vegetable nature, where the Mandragora, properly approached, can cast a spell, where poetry makes a chill run up your spine: the mother, the son of the mother, the son of the son.

We are driving through the very plain of Thrace from which Dan called me a year ago. From the car we watch the sun set into a high bank of deep blue clouds and emerge again as though reborn, only to die again in more clouds and earth, but it keeps throwing light onto the fringes of cloud, making great diagonals of blue into the darkening sky. It keeps on, this death and birth and death again. Krassy murmurs: "the son of the sun!"

What mystery is it that was revealed on this journey? Is it about Semele, earth mother, whom it is said danced when she was pregnant with Dionysus, and the child within her, danced also? Is it about Dionysus and the experience of fragmentation, because poetry, as I am coming to understand, is made up of what Pound calls "luminous fragments," the distillation of experience and emotion into charged pieces of language that don't necessarily make cognitive sense but touch down to something deeper.

Why has Dionysus insinuated himself into my consciousness, transported me to Thrace, sent me on a wild goose chase to find him, sent a centaur in

---

136 Fol, *The Thracian Dionysius*, Book Two, p. 312.

his stead? But Dionysus does not respond to the question "why." He is about living experience, the kind that cracks you open, that takes you down to your elemental nature. A veil rips, and suddenly I see what seems so obvious: Dionysus has been with me for this whole journey, sending shivers of Kundalini energy up my spine, taking me places I didn't know I needed to go, showing me gods I didn't know I needed to know, introducing me to my Muse in unknown forms, as maenad, as root vegetable, as centaur.

Perhaps the mystery that has been revealed is about Cheiron, this newly emerging figure in my psyche. I turn to him, in active imagination, and ask whether it is he who has been whispering in my ear all these years, of Semele, of Dionysus, of Thrace.

No, he says, don't over interpret me. I am just another fragment of the deep pattern of which you can never see the whole. I don't appear until you're ready for the mystery. But once you've seen me, I stay with you. I live in the Thracian glade, and I live in your heart. Green leaves cover my body. I am life that goes on forever. I am healing. I am joy. I am the place where the wild and the cultured meet. I am the beginning of culture, cultivating the knowledge of herbs, of roots, of the wisdom of dreams. I am centaur, wild irrepressible animal instinct, pure phallic abandon. And I am Cheiron, matured, married, wounded. I am the horse of your girlhood, steed of poetic imagination. And I am the blend of animal instinct, human head and hands you need to carry you through the ecstasies of creativity, the mysteries of a deeply lived life.

I wrote a poem about this journey, in which I threaded together some of the most numinous fragments:

Mystery

> *this never happened but it always is*
> —Salustius

something is gathering
out of what ocean whispered
              all night
                    to the rocks
out of what was revealed
                in the dark of the cave
out of a place i've not yet been

but always am—
woods where the old gods speak—

time arrives
bedraggled and luminous
here
in the Sheraton Sofia

animal claws under the hotel table
are about to leap out the arched window
unto the verdigris dome of the old church—
Sveta Nedalya—
where pigeons roost
upon whose steps the bride is
about to be kissed by a little girl
bearing rosebuds

and in the museum
we have seen the Varna Necropolis
king who died four millenia ago
gold discs around his head
golden penis sheath
golden navel of the world
and the bird headed goddess
whose name is Helena

something is soon to be
gathered
in rolling blue mountains
that call themselves Thrace—
broken cooking vessel
peak we couldn't climb
girl friend with glowing red hair
i lost in a pocket of sobbing
from childhood
(when did she return?)
we walk among muttering stones
we are almost old

what mystery is it
that what tore us apart
remembers us back
among springs and old groves

on animal hooves and covered with grape leaves?
we are carried away to some mountain altar
      where

            fire in the dark
            drum beat of heart
            quickening leap of the god—
            who never has been
                but always is—
              dances
                    behind closed
                      eyelids[137]

---

137 Lowinsky, *Psychological Perspectives,* Issue 45, 2003.

The Book of Ruth: Naomi's Version

The Sound of My Name

Who can comprehend the mysteries of naming? My parents named me Naomi Ruth. My father, a musicologist, said he liked the musical sound of the name. As a girl I wanted an ordinary name, a regular American name like Carol or Judy. Naomi Ruth felt too big, too foreign. Then, at twelve, entering puberty, a boy in my seventh grade class had a way of saying my name, "Na Oh mi," that stirred me strangely. Walking down a crowded hall full of laughing, teasing teenagers, I would hear my name being sung like an ancient song, "Na Oh mi." I did want to be that Na Oh mi he was calling. I couldn't stop thinking about that boy in my seventh grade class. Was it a crush? Or an early stirring of the meaning of my name?

But my parents called my Ne ohm, and my friends called me Nayomi or Niyome and we moved to California and no one called me Na Oh mi. I was a divorced mother of three in my mid-thirties before anyone called me Na Oh mi again and that man became my husband. Years later, when we traveled to Israel, I learned that what my soul responded to was the Hebraic pronunciation of my name, as though the muse of my own people spoke to me through that sound. Though Na Oh mi is quickly and commonly elided into Nomi in Israel, the truest, grandest most ancient pronunciation of my name is the one that moved me so deeply when I was twelve.

It surprised me greatly to learn that I had such a powerful response to the Hebrew sound of my name, for my connection to Judaism has been deeply conflicted. For most of my conscious life I have been wrestling with the desacralization of the feminine principle in Judaism, the prohibition against the graven image and the jealous nature of that abstract god who wants us to have no other gods before him. I love gods and goddesses. In India as a young woman I responded spiritually, soulfully, sensuously to the rich pantheon of gods and goddesses, and their graven images: baby Krishna stealing the butterball, Shakti and Shiva making love, dancing Ganesha with his elephant head, Kali bringing you into life and taking you out in one fell swoop of her bony arms. I have graven images of these gods and goddesses in my home and in my office. I love imagery and have followed with much excitement the emergence of ancient goddess imagery during my lifetime. It is as though the feminine is returning to our consciousness.

The psychological struggle within me to give voice to what felt taboo in Judaism, to honor images of the goddess, was expressed by a dream I had years ago, when I was just beginning to talk publicly about her. In the dream I am preparing to give a talk on the goddess, when a rabbi strides past me on his way to the podium. He is heading up there to steal my talk. I run to get there first, but he's way ahead of me. There he stands, in his long black robes, facing my audience. He begins to talk, a banal, boring talk. I am going to have to make a scene, which is not something I like to do, even in my dreams. Interrupting him, I say: "Excuse me, this is my talk!" Surprisingly he gives little resistance. He shrugs, and gets down off the podium.

Dealing with the Old Testament hasn't been so easy. The Ten Commandments, for example, forbid the worship of graven images. In *Exodus* it is written:

> Thou shalt have no other gods before me.
> Thou shalt not make unto thee any graven image, or any likeness of any thing that is in heaven above, or that is in the earth beneath, or that is in the water under the earth:
> Thou shalt not bow down thyself to them, nor serve them: for I the Lord thy God am a jealous God...[138]

Moses received this commandment among others from the God of the Jews on his way to the Promised Land. But when he came back down from the mountain he saw his people worshiping a graven image, the Golden Calf. In *Exodus* it is written that Moses:

> saw the calf, and the dancing: and Moses' anger waxed hot, and he cast the tables out of his hands, and brake them beneath the mount. And he took the calf which they had made, and burnt it in the fire, and ground it to powder...[139]

A poem came to me. It began with a dream. A woman in blue pajamas is visited by a vision, an energy that pulls at her left eye and insists she look at red clay. The red clay compelled me, reminded me of the red blood of the goddess of which Adam was created. After weeks of wrestling with words and images, that red clay dropped me down to the ancient conflict in my soul

---

138 *The King James Bible*, Exodus 20:3-5.
139 *The King James Bible*, Exodus 32:19-20.

between Moses and the graven image: the Golden Calf. The calf or the bull was sacred in the Great Mother traditions because, the horns and head of the bull are the shape of the uterus and fallopian tubes.[140] This poem took me over, insisted its way through me, until I began to understand the meaning of that Golden Calf, and the old religion, the religion of the goddess. Here is the poem:

red clay is talking

a woman
in blue pajamas
is being visited
by a vision

red clay is talking to her
it's talking about genesis
it's talking about images
it's showing her an ancient way to shape a god

> it's tugging at her left eye.
> she can't focus
> her house is such
>
> > a commotion

the men come in
they're hungry
she cannot find
her writing book
her mother
has had a revelation
she needs to tell the whole story

> the woman can't get past
> > the table
> > littered with demands
> > for money
> she can't get past
> > the petrified
> > blond child

---

140 Buffie Johnson, *Lady of the Beasts*, p. 272.

with tight braids
she once was—

unless the men
get fed
the mother
heard
the money
made

all hell is about
      to burst—
      she can just see

the weeping
   in blue pajamas
      the shattering
      of the beloved
      image
      in the desert—

don't you remember?
her vision is speaking
before the breaking of the tablets
      of the law—

      you were the one
      who wore the yellow robes
      who took the gods into your hands—

      digging deep
      stirring the blood and milk into
                       red clay

      making a horned calf to shine
    in the image of a woman's
          holy place—

they said that it was gold
   that moved you
   they did not understand
   you melted down your jewels
      to give a form to

mystery—
    the horned fallopian
    the bowl of sacrifice
    the delta of the wordless one
        dreaming the inward sea—

forbidden by the prophet
he's found a god
who leaps about the mind
forsaking what the body knows
this god
        engraves blood law
        into a stone
        and leaves you empty
            as a horned moon—

a woman in blue pajamas
calls out to her vision
    "come back
    tell me the story of those other gods"

    red clay is talking to her
    "take me in your hands
    hold me
    knead me
    make me in the shape of the animal you are

    and i will tell the fingers of your grasp
    the fate line of your palm
    the scatter and break of the mark of your heart
        the secret godforsaken story"[141]

The Secret Godforsaken Story

It was in a workshop with the Israeli Jungian analyst Rachel Hillel that I learned that the "secret godforsaken story," the story of the loss and the redemption of the feminine principle in Judaism, is told, somewhat covertly, in none other than the *Book of Ruth*![142]

---

141 Lowinsky, *red clay is talking*, p. 122.
142 Rachel Hillel, *The Redemption of the Feminine Erotic Soul*.

Rachel Hillel told the story that the red clay tells in my poem, the story of forsaken genesis, the story of those other gods. For when the new monotheistic masculine consciousness entered Judaism, something of the feminine principle was lost. The land became barren. The goddess of the earth, like Demeter in her deep depression after the loss of Persephone, stopped being fruitful and there was a terrible famine.

When Naomi and her family go to Moab, according to Rachel Hillel, they are traveling to a Canaanite land where the goddess was still worshipped. At last I understood, many years after my parents named me, the mythic meaning of my name! I was named for the ancient Naomi, who made the journey back into the polytheistic goddess traditions, and returned with a young woman who had been raised in that tradition, and who brought the feminine principle back into Judaism. Many Jungians have told this story, beginning with Yechezkel Kluger and including Edward Edinger and Ann Ulanov.

The *Book of Ruth* is set in the time just after the Jews enter Canaan, the Promised Land, the land of milk and honey, under the leadership of Joshua. It was a time of enormous religious turmoil and spiritual confusion. The first line of the book reads: "Now it came to pass in the days when the judges ruled…" Its placement in the Bible is right after the *Book of Judges*. It can be seen as a personal story, a small detailed miniature version of the epic drama that Judges describes with a much broader brush stroke. The *Book of Judges* gives us the context for the *Book of Ruth*. It describes the wars between the children of Israel and the Canaanites, while they were engaged in taking over the Promised Land. Then, as now, the Promised Land was no empty vessel waiting to be filled. It was full of indigenous people with their own gods and goddesses. This is the way it is told in the *Book of Judges*:

> And the children of Israel dwelt among the Canaanites, Hittites, and Amorites and Perizzites and Hivites and Jebusites:
> And they took their daughters to be their wives, and gave their daughters to their sons, and served their gods.
> And the children of Israel did evil in the sight of the Lord, and forgat the Lord their God, and served Baalim and the groves.
> And the children of Israel did evil again in the sight of the Lord . . . and they forsook the Lord and served Baal and Ashtaroth.[143]

---

143 *The King James Bible*, Judges 3:5-7; 2:11, 2:13.

Who are the Baalim, and who is this Ashtaroth? In his seminal book, *The Hebrew Goddess,* Raphael Patai writes:

> . . . to the very end of the Hebrew Monarchy the worship of old Canaanite gods was an integral part of the religion of the Hebrews . . . The image of Yahweh, in the eyes of the common people, did not differ greatly from that of Baal or the other Canaanite male gods . . . The worship of Yahweh thus easily merged into, complemented, or supplanted that of the Canaanite male gods.
>
> But Yahwism lacked the female touch which was such an important part of Canaanite religious life. Nothing it could offer replaced the Canaanite goddesses. Therefore, the prophetic denunciations of these idols had little effect . . .[144]

Patai goes on to say that the Hebrews took over the worship of the fertility goddess Asherah from the Canaanites. The goddess "was represented by carved wooden images implanted into the ground . . . and located on hilltops, under leafy trees." The goddess also took the form of small clay figurines. These were for the private use of women, who invoked her help in childbirth.[145]

Elinor Gadon, author of *The Once and Future Goddess* imagines this time in the following way:

> Yahweh, the god of the Israelites, was born in the milieu of herders and context of the desert. He was not tied to a sanctuary, to a sacred site, or the land but to a group of men....When the small group that had been led by Moses entered Canaan under the leadership of Joshua (ca.1200), they made war in the name of Yahweh, converting other tribes. But the religion of the people of the land, firmly rooted in practices sacred to an agricultural way of life, was not easily displaced.[146]

Gadon goes on to speak of the power of the graven image:

> . . . as far back as the Paleolithic the Goddess had been worshiped through votive images in the shape of the body of the Goddess. They were small enough to fit into a clasping hand; devotion was sensual. The most commonly used medium was clay, the very earth that is her body . . . to prohibit the making of the Goddess image is to disembody her, to sever her from her life force, which is the earth.[147]

---

144 Raphael Patai, *The Hebrew Goddess,* p. 31.
145 Patai, *The Hebrew Goddess,* p. 45.
146 Elinor Gadon, *The Once and Future Goddess,* p. 181.
147 Gadon, *The Once and Future Goddess,* p. 184.

The "*Ur* Naomi": A Visitation

In the dark of the bottom of the year, right after the winter solstice, I sat on my poetry porch, a little glassed-in corner off the bedroom with a soft green view of hills and valleys and the San Pablo Reservoir off in the distance, to meditate upon the *Book of Ruth*. Suddenly, as though she has been waiting for this moment all my life, the ancient Naomi welled up in me like a dark song that is a river—a song of lament that has always flowed under the earth of my being. She appeared in the eyes of my imagination in the body of a woman who makes no apology for being female and for having lived a hard life. Hers is the face of one who has suffered many losses, been tempered by many experiences, traveled far, and not been afraid to look at difficult truths. Her eyes have laughter in them, and irony, and an objectivity that can be ruthless.

She told me she was the "*Ur* Naomi," using that wonderful German word which means old, primitive, ancient. She makes it clear that she was a very different Naomi from the small-time Naomi I am, who lives in this body, in this time, this psychology, and who has struggled in her small life and limited vision with the God of the Jews. *Ur* Naomi sees the whole picture—the spiritual story of Jewish women for the last three thousand years. She is "*das Urbild*" the archetype of the crone in her Jewish cultural vestment. That morning, on my poetry porch, she announced that I was to write her version of the *Book of Ruth*.

"But wait a minute," I said, "I'm no biblical scholar. How can I do that?"

You're no scholar of any sort!

She gives me her look of absolute objectivity.

You don't need to be a scholar. The scholars have done their work. You've read some of them. Your job is a poet's job. The poets have always focused on Ruth's experience as a stranger in a strange land. But I too was a stranger, and I too have a story. It's the old woman's story that most needs telling, for that's the story that's always left out. You're old enough now to begin to imagine me. I want you to tell my version of the Book of Ruth.

My story was told for hundreds of years before it was written down. It is a woman's story, told by women, for women and for men. It is a story of ordinary people, told by ordinary people to ordinary people. In those days, women singers—poets or story tellers you would call them today—would walk from village to village, singing their tales.[148] But when the stories began to be written down, it was only men who learned the carving of the words into stone. The men who wrote my story down in the bible had a political purpose. It was a worthy purpose, what you call "politically correct" these days. They told my story as a way to support intermarriage and to take a stand against those zealots in the land who said there was only one true god; who wanted to outlaw any signs of the old religion with all of its gods and goddesses. What hurts my heart is that they would not write the deeper story down. They had to hide it in symbolism which the people of that time understood, but the people of your time have forgotten. So I will tell you the "secret story," the story under the story.

When I was a girl my mother told me there was a secret in my name. It meant "winsome," it meant "my lovely one," but it was also an old name from the Canaanite people that meant "delight of the gods."[149] My mother missed the old religion of her mother's mother, the graven images that were now forbidden to us in Judea. She gave me a name that would be the story of my life, for it was my fate to go out to the land where people still knew these gods and goddesses, and it was my fate to bring them back to my people. But I am getting ahead of myself.

A bad time came to the land of Bethlehem Judea, a time of famine, a dry time, the time of the troubles, when women turned against women, and men against men, for nothing would grow in the fields and there was not enough food to go around. I was young then, hardly more than a girl, but married, as was the custom, the mother of two sons, named Mahlon and Chilion. Later their names would haunt me, for Mahlon means "weakening and pining," and Chilion means "blot out and perish."[150]

My husband, Elimelech was a good man, loyal, but stubborn. His name, Elimelech, which means "my God is king"[151] suited him, for he followed the new god, the nameless one. This new god, for whom my husband was named, was a god of the desert and of the wind. He was not a god who understood the slow cycles of the fruits of the earth. Something was wrong in the land of Judea, especially with the women. They were drying up—many were barren.

---

148   Edward Campbell, *The Anchor Bible: Ruth*, p. 23.
149   *The Anchor Bible: Ruth*, p. 53.
150   Ruth Sasson in Robert Alter and Frank Kermode, *The Literary Guide to the Bible*, p. 322.
151   *The Anchor Bible: Ruth*, p. 52.

My own mother-in-law, with whom I had to live, became strange—as women do who live too close to the sound of the wind. A woman cannot tolerate too much wind. It can blow her soul away. And the crops, that must be buried deep in the earth as seed is buried in the body of woman, became as crazy as the women. They lost their hold on the land. Things blew every which way. My mother-in-law blew in and out of the kitchen—she had no resting place, she could not sit still. She could not cook. She could not hold her grandsons and soothe them. They cried and cried in her arms. I said to my husband, "Elimelech, we must go. We must leave this land for there is a crazy wind upon it." What I did not say was, I cannot live with your mother. I cannot hand her our children.

My husband Elimelech said, "How can I leave the land of my people and your people? How can I leave the house in which our sons were born? How can I leave the god to whom I have been consecrated?"

"How can you not," said I ? "Your god is not feeding us. The gods of the earth are angry."

What could he say? He knew I was right. I left the house of my mother-in-law, and walked with my husband and my sons to another land, a strange land, the land of Moab. Here the people still worshipped the old gods, in the form of graven images which had been forbidden in the land of Judea. My mother had told me of these gods, some made of wood, some made of clay. She said they helped a woman in her time of labor. She said that there was one, Anath, whose name meant "She of the Womb."

In this land I was a stranger at the well, a stranger among the Moabite women whose gods were forbidden by the god of my husband. They knew that I came from the land of the nameless god and at first I could tell that they feared me. They had heard of our leader Samuel, who destroyed all the Baalim and Ashtaroth among us, and in the name of the nameless god, led our people to great victories over those who worshipped idols.

I watched the Moabite women from a distance. I was curious. I was lonely. I watched as they gathered at the altar on a hilltop to worship their Asherah. I watched them make music and dance. I learned that there was a fall festival where the women gathered and no man was allowed, not even a male dog. I heard it was a festival to consecrate their bleeding.[152] I heard that in the

---

152 Betty de Shong Meador, "The Thesmophoria: A Woman's Ritual." *Psychological Perspectives*, Vol. 17 no. 1, 1986.

temples the priestesses trained the young women in the ways of love. They were called hetaera and were practiced in the arts of music, dance and poetry. They celebrated women's blood and milk and sexual joy. They made graven images with breasts and full bellies. They baked cakes in the shape of the vulva and ate them!

After a season had passed, and the women of Moab had grown accustomed to the sight of me going to the well for water in the mornings and the evenings, some of them befriended me. They took me to be blessed by their Asherah. She was tall and lovely and carved out of wood. Her feet were pushed into the ground like a tree. They took me to their homes where each woman had her own altar. They showed me how to form a goddess out of clay, how to make her breasts, how to shape her vulva, how to paint her red in the color of a woman's blood.

And though I missed my people, especially my mother and my father, I lived a different life in Moab than I would have in Bethlehem Judea. I was given the gift of forbidden pleasure, forbidden gods, forbidden feelings, greater range for my thoughts and my prayers. For I prayed not only to the god of the Jews but to the goddess, the Asherah and her daughter Anath—She of the Womb. I set up a small altar in my kitchen and made a graven image. She was so beautiful. Her hair was like green ferns after a rain. Her hands held up her breasts. Her vulva was pronounced and sacred. My husband, however, was not happy in this place. It made him uneasy. The gods of the Moabites were an abomination to him. He said our god, the god of the Jews, had no name and had no shape, and was neither male or female.

I said, "Nonsense, we all know he's a he. Every name you call his name-lessness is a masculine word. And anyway, only a man could imagine a god without a body. No woman who knows the tug of her blood, the swelling of her belly with child, the tug of her child's mouth on her breast, could imagine a god without a body."

Elimelech said, "Our god is a jealous god and wants us to forsake all other gods and worship only him." But I needed those other gods. How could I get him to understand that to touch a shape outside myself—that is like my shape, or the shape of what is within me—makes me feel whole? It is the carnal knowledge of myself that allows me to feel the goddess within. I am the mortal shape of "She of the Womb," as was my mother, and her mother before her.

Elimelech said I was worshipping idols, material things, that the god of the Jews was a god of the wind, of the spirit, not of the earth.

I said, "What is breath without body, what is spirit without soul, what is wind without earth? Your wind god blew and roared and wandered and loosened the earth from its moorings, made sand of it, made desert of it, and there was no water. There was no heaviness of body, no dropping down of ache like a woman before her menstrual period. And so the land grew barren as a woman without her blood cycle. For the god of the Jews has no mother, no wife, no children, and the god of the Jews tears up the red earth and forsakes the old religion of the womb."

Elimelech said, "It is too much about women here—blood of the women, milk of the women, heads of the bull in the shape of a woman's womb. Women's things. A man gets lost in all the confusion of the blood and the milk. Our people went with Abraham to leave all that behind, to make the leap to a higher consciousness in which god is an idea, not a body, not a material thing, a consciousness about law, not just about the urges of the body or the cycle of the harvest."

He said the Moabites were the children of Lot whose daughter seduced him. They are the children of incest which is forbidden by our god. I said, "Lot's daughter had a problem. There were no other men to marry. Their people were going to die out. And look what happened. She seduced her father and here is this vibrant living culture, the fruits of her valor." He said, "The men among these people have no contract with their God. They do not know the power of the law that Moses brought down from the mountain. How can their lives have meaning?" And so we would argue.

I knew the land of Moab was not good for Elimelech. I could feel his soul getting moldy amidst all the wet stuff of the women, the mixing of the blood and the milk, the seething of a kid in its mother's milk. He longed for his desert god. I could feel his spirit rotting, and after a few years, with our sons just blooming into young men, Elimelech died.

And though I grieved and felt alone without him, I had my two fine sons, and many friends among the Canaanite women. And my friends came to me and said, "It is time your sons took wives." And they chose among their daughters Orpah and Ruth, two of the loveliest and the best educated. For the women of Moab were educated in the temples of the priestesses of love. And what they meant by knowledge was carnal knowledge, of their own bodies, their own ecstasy, and how to give pleasure to a man. I think my friends thought that the men of Judah were lacking the power of the baalim, the male gods, for they said, "How could a god without a body fill a young husband with the proper joy?

Such a man, whose god has no name and no body, would need a joy maiden to show him the way of love." The joy maidens were trained in the healing of men who were not in harmony with their bodies.

I was grateful for Orpah and Ruth. For the first time since I was a girl with a mother and sisters, I lived in a house filled with women. I was good to them and did not rule over them ruthlessly as many mothers-in-law do, as vengeance for the time when they were young and under the thumb of a mother-in-law. My daughters-in-law introduced me to the rituals of the Moabite women. They took me into their temples. They took me out to the fields in November and made me a member of their mystery rituals. I learned the meaning of the mixing of the blood and the milk; I participated in the secret ritual in which a kid is seethed in its mother's milk, a ritual so sacred no one can speak of it, except the Hebrew prophet who made it a commandment that no Jew shall seethe a kid in its mother's milk.

I would not have left the land of Moab. I was full there. I had sons. I had daughters-in-law. There was cooking and the laughter of women in my kitchen. And though I slept alone, a widow, I heard the laughter and the teasing between my sons and their wives and I was glad. I waited for grandchildren. They never came, my grandchildren. For something was wrong here too, here in Moab. I heard the voice of my husband, Elimelech, may he rest in peace, saying, "Too much about women here, too much blood, too much milk, too much seething a kid in its mother's milk." We had argued about these things in life. After his death I learned to hear his point of view.

Among the Moabites they said a good husband was a good Baal—a good ploughman, a fructifier of his woman. My husband had scoffed at this. "Their heads are in their uncircumcised penises," he said. "They have no contract with God, only with earth and with women." And I heard my friends, the women of Moab, wondering about my sons. What was wrong with them? Ten years of marriage and no grandchildren.

And now came another bad time, a terrible time. And I who had been full became empty; I who had been sweet became bitter. For although I flourished in the land of Moab in the company of my daughters-in-law, my sons did not. And I could see that the souls of my sons were rotting in the land of women's ways, in the shadow of "She of the Womb." They were lost without their father and his dry desert god. And so Mahlon, whose name means "weakening and pining" and Chilion whose name means "blot out and perish," became sick and died. And I heard my husband's voice bewailing the fate of his sons and I knew my time in the land of Moab was coming to an end.

Intreat Me Not to Leave You

My parents had called me Naomi, sweet one, delight of the gods. Secretly, my mother had given me as a gift to the goddess. Was it my mother's longing for the old gods that sent me wandering to the land of Moab? Was it this lust for the old gods, for the women's ways that mix the blood and the milk, that killed my husband and my sons? I was no longer my mother's Naomi, nor Elimelech's joy nor Asherah's delight. I turned to my daughters–in–law and said, "Call me Mara for I have been cast into darkness and my name means bitter one. The nameless god of my husband has lifted his hand against me, and the gods of the old religion have forsaken me. El and his Asherah have robbed me and you of the pleasures of marriage, and Anath, She of the Womb, has denied me grand-children." And I said to Orpah and Ruth, now widowed like I was, "Though I left the land of my people, and came to Moab where I found great solace among you women and your gods, I can see that is not the end of my journey. The voice of my husband, Elimelech, rings in my ears, telling me I must leave this place. He says there is a better harvest now among my kinfolk in Judea. He says that there is much that I must still experience among my own people, and with my husband's God. Go back my daughters, to the homes of your mothers, to the temples of your goddess, to the sacred groves of your Asherah."

And Orpah, whose soul shines in her eyes like a great flower in the morning light, cried out, "But Mother, you will be alone. No one will know your story or remember your life. We knew your husband Elimelech. We knew your sons. I have the touch of Chilion on my body still. I remember him. Who will remem-ber what you loved and how you lived if you go back alone to Judea? We will come with you. We will remember your menfolk."

I said, "My daughters, you are still young. You can still bear children. Your bodies are like lovely fields that need to be ploughed for you've never born fruit. But I have no more sons to marry you. If you come with me to Judea who will you marry? You are women of Moab, where the men know how to be good Baa-lim. Can a man of my people serve you in that way?"

And I saw Orpah's soul sink into darkness. And she wept, for she knew I was right. She needed to stay among her people and her gods, but it tore at her heart. It is terrible to know that it is the end of a time, the end of a family, the end of a line. But she knew the truth when she heard it. And so she embraced us, and wept again, and lifted up her skirts and ran to her mother's house.

I expected Ruth to do the same thing, except with fewer words, for she was quieter than Orpah. Her light burned from an inward place. But Ruth did not go. She put her hands on my shoulders and passion filled her lovely young body and her voice when she said, "We belong to each other. We are part of the same story. My destiny awaits me among your people, I can feel its pull. Intreat me not to leave you, or to return from following after you. Your people shall be my people, your gods shall be my gods, your fate shall be my fate. Where you die I will die, and there will I be buried."

What could I say? She was sure this was her path. I feared for her what I feared for myself—an un-befriended, hungry, barren widowhood. When the poet Keats imagines the song of the nightingale piercing Ruth's heart as she stands, "sick for home amid the alien corn," that was my fear for her. For I had known what it was to be a stranger in a strange land. I feared she would miss the women's ways of her mother, her sisters and her friends. And Ruth said, "We will take with us our Asherah, and our household gods, and our graven images of clay, to hold in our hands and help us find our way."

So it was that I arrived in Bethlehem Judea with Ruth, the Moabitess. It was the beginning of the barley harvest. And as I approached the well where I had drawn water as a girl, the women gathered, murmured and wondered who were these foreigners. And someone cried out, "Can that be Naomi? Look, how changed she is!" And I said to the women of my homeland, just as I had said to my daughters–in–law, "Do not call me Naomi, call me Mara, for the gods have dealt bitterly with me, and the god of Judea has testified against me and afflicted me." And I told the women the story of my sojourn among the Moabites, and how full I had been, and now how empty.

I asked the women about my kinfolk. And the women told me of the death of my parents, and the parents of Elimelech. They said that there was one among the family of my husband who might be a redeemer. His name was Boaz, which means man of strength, and his wife had just died, and left him alone. He was a landowner whose fields were being harvested.

And Ruth said to me, "Mother, let me go to the fields and glean so that we may have food, and so this Boaz may see me." And I knew what she was doing, priestess trained as she was. And the goddess was with her and it was her luck that took her to the field which belonged to Boaz. And Boaz' eyes alit upon her, for she was lovely to see, and a light burned within her. And Boaz asked his servant about her and was told that she was with me and had come back with me from the land of Moab. And Boaz spoke to Ruth, and told her to glean only in his fields, for he had told the young men to keep their hands off her, and to give her water to drink when she was thirsty. And Boaz gave her to eat and to drink, and praised her for her loyalty to me. And when she returned in the evening she had beat out a full measure of barley, and I knew that we would not go hungry. And so she stayed among the maidens of Boaz, and gleaned in the barley harvest, and in the wheat harvest.

You know the story of what happens next, that I speak to Ruth and tell her that Boaz, our kinsman, will be winnowing barley on the threshing floor. I tell her to wash herself, and anoint herself, and put on her best garments, and go to him while he sleeps. When the women singers told this part of the story, the people knew what they meant. What do you think it means, when I tell her to uncover Boaz's leg? You think I mean his leg? You know what I mean. She knew what I meant. She was not trained in the erotic arts by the priestess for nothing!

And the threshing floor, what is that all about? We all know the obvious meaning, it's where the wheat and the barley are threshed. But in the tradition of the old religion, the threshing floor was where the sacred marriage was enacted. Right there on the ground, amidst the fruit of the harvest, the priestess and the priest would enact the sacred marriage so that the fields would would give a plentiful harvest.

Ruth knew what she was doing, bringing the erotic arts back to the land of the Jews. Boaz knew what she was doing. He was no judge or prophet who would condemn her, who would tear down the sacred groves of Asherah. He knew that what the land needed was the deep red power of the woman and he honored it in Ruth. Yet he did not go into her that night on the threshing floor. He knew that redemption required that he stay within the law.

For my kinsman, Boaz, was a crafty one. He knew what he wanted, but he did not leap, he planned. He acted on my behalf, on Elimelech and Mahlon's behalf, and on Ruth's behalf. He spread his skirt over Ruth and told her to sleep, and in the morning he would talk to one who was even a nearer kinsman than he.

When I heard from the women at the well, and from Ruth, what Boaz had done, I felt my kinship with him, I heard the voice of Elimelech—"Circumcision is a contract with God. A man who has made this contract does not act directly from his penis. For it belongs to God before it belongs to what you desire. You must wait, and act according to the law of redemption." And so Boaz made his crafty plan, and he made it clear to the nearer kinsman that if he claimed my land, the land of Elimelech, he would lose it in the end because Boaz would act the part of the redeemer with Ruth, and thus Mahlon's son would get the land in the end. And Boaz played more than the part of the kinsman, he played the part of a greater redeemer than even was required. For he looked upon Ruth with the eyes of love and took her as his wife. And he turned out to be a good Baal, for she conceived a child.

Yet it did not go easily, this marriage of a priestess trained Moabitess with a man of Judea. He died shortly after the wedding, and left her a widow again, only this time with child. But the women of Judea were overjoyed to have their Asherah back. And we made a place for the goddess on a hill near the well. And we decorated her and gave her offerings of food and drink. And when her time came Ruth held in her hand a small clay image of Anath, "She of the Womb," and it gave her strength in her labor, and brought comfort to her body and her soul, and her son was born whole.

And the goddess was with me and with Ruth. She put the child Obed, into my arms, and lo, a miracle happened. I held my grandson and the milk sprang into my breast. I, an old woman, past the time of childbearing, had milk to spare and I became his nurse. And the women cried out: "Lo a miracle, for a son has been born to Naomi."[153]

And Obed was the father of Jesse, and Jesse was the father of David. That is the story the men tell in the written word. But I have told you the story of the other gods, the secret story of the Book of Ruth, the story of gods forsaken and gods redeemed, the story of how the goddess came back to the land of Judea. And the women held her sacred, and prayed to her about the matters of their blood and their milk, their lovemaking and their birthgiving and held her graven images in their hands when their time came. And the children of Obed and Jesse and David honored the goddess. And Solomon brought her golden serpent back into the temple because he honored his Sidonian wife. And so it was for hundreds of years, though the judges judged, and the prophets raged. We Jewish women had our graven images at home and in the temple the nameless

---

153 *The King James Bible*, Ruth 4:17

one, blessed be he, cohabitated with the snake goddess all decked out in gold. The goddess is not jealous. She likes lots of gods. She was happy to live with the nameless one. Those were the years of plenty.

After the destruction of the temple in Jerusalem, after the death of the spirit of idolatry, the Goddess that Ruth and I had brought back to Judaism went underground, like a forgotten river, like the ancient lament of the mothers, like Lilith's shrieking on the Day of Atonement, alone in the wilderness by the red sea. She was called the Great Whore of Babylon and feared as the source of all evil.

She went into the land of dreams, into the mystical traditions of Judaism, into Gnosticism as Sophia, into the Kabbalah as the Shekinah, and into the hermetic alchemical tradition as the Soror Mystica.

So you see, (and the "Ur Naomi" gave me her ironic, objective look) you were named for a 3000 year old female energy in Judaism that's been seeking to bring the erotic, embodied, life giving female principle back to Western consciousness. I know there are many of you, in your time, who have been working in my name. But it's not only the female principle that has been missing; it is the embodied male principle, the Boaz, who could join with Ruth in a marriage of equal partners. That is the work of the future.

So it was that I came to understand the meaning of my name and of my myth, and why my dreams and poems were frequented by pagan priestesses and goddesses. The *Ur Naomi* connects me to the essence of who I am, as in the poem I call, "in the real story."

in the real story

you are a dancing girl
a devadesi from the temple at Jaipur
or maybe it is Ur
the sacred fire's been lit
i've taught you how
to catch your own sweet pulse—

      you await the stranger
      who crosses the desert
            on a red mare
      two moons this night
      your hands on his back
      your soles on the stones
      you drink
            the milky way

      in the real story
      your open thighs reveal
          the crescent
              moon[154]

---

154 Lowinsky, *crimes of the dreamer*, p. 27.

Beloved of the Beloved

I am a most fleshly fire.
I would embrace you in that flame...
                —Robert Duncan[155]

Male Muse

Creative work is erotic. It's exciting, a turn-on; when the writing is going well I feel physically aroused. I have been initiated into my life as a poet by a series of inner figures, most of whom have been female. She forces herself into my consciousness and has her way. Or, in another mood, another mode, She eludes me, shimmers at the edges of memory, fills me with yearning. She lures me into other dimensions, haunts, remembers me back to my ancestors and my most ancient Self. She lights the fire of my erotic imagination, which is essential to all creative work. She is lover and beloved, high priestess and goddess, me and not me. She has shaken up my life and returned me to soul. She considers me, quite rightly, her own.

Then suddenly, surprisingly, a masculine voice comes to consciousness. He probes. He questions. He wonders whether I'm not leaving something out.

I wonder, what would that be?

He responds, *Me. Your male Muse. Where is it written that the Muse is always female? Or that the flow of libido is only about the energy between a woman and her goddess? What of the erotic between male and female? What of Inanna and Damuzi? What of Shiva and Shakti? Even in the goddess religions there comes a time when the sexes are united, when the god and the goddess, the priest and the priestess are joined. In the Eleusinian Mysteries, in Tantric Yoga, in Dionysian revels and the pagan practices of Old Europe, the union of male and female is sacred. When the angel comes to Mary, he is announcing a mystical union between a male god and a mortal woman, out of which the divine child is born. How can you write of the creative and ignore me?*

He is making me nervous. I can't really argue with him. It sounds true enough. But my generation of women has had a tremendous struggle emerg-

155 Robert Duncan, *Selected Poems*, p. 7.

ing out of male definitions to find a deep and female sense of self. The feminine has been numinous for many of us. The connection to the goddess has opened the floodgates to my creative life. She has touched me and given me the gift of feeling whole.

It's hard not to be suspicious of this male voice. If I trust him, will he remove me from myself? I'm suddenly flooded by a memory. It begins so sweetly: my father has tucked me into bed, stroked my hair, kissed my forehead. And then he carefully places my hands outside the covers. A chill runs through my body—a kind of dread. The message is clear: thou shalt not play with thyself! It took years to understand, in a bodily sense, that there is no creativity that is not playing with oneself. This is not the creativity understood by the brilliant scholarly mind of a man like my father. It springs out of the deep feminine, meanders the soft inwardness of a woman's body, the slow labyrinthine turnings of her soul. I have learned not to listen to the male energy in me that wants to know where I'm headed, what the bottom line is, what is the point of all this inwardness. It cuts me off from myself.

That's not who I am, says this one who claims to be my muse. *I've been around forever, from the time before writing. Don't you remember the trail of dreams I've left in your life? I've showed up as shaman, as ecstatic rabbi, as Thanksgiving poet, as grandfather. I am the one who walks in the river to its source. I am that bearded young poet who showed you a garden full of glowing crystals. I am the gardener who knows how to prune the flowering fruit trees.*

And so he talks, an insistent voice in my head. He claims that without his guidance, his presence, no writing would happen. He wants me to be conscious of him, to invite him in, to return his love. Is he to be trusted? Or is he some split off aspect of the patriarchy, some member of the committee of judges who cannot see the feminine as complete within herself? Is this a seduction or a trustworthy reassurance that it's safe to let the masculine in? Am I supposed to listen to the mocking voice?

Are you saying your male muse is some sort of sensitive new age guy? I suppose he goes out and drums in the woods. Next you'll be talking about the green man, the phallic tree that pierces the sky, the phallic root that pierces the ground? There's nothing new in that. Your colleagues have been writing about the chthonic masculine for years.

This is a painfully familiar voice. It always feels male to me and is why I distrust the so-called male muse. He's likely to turn into the judge, the critic at any moment, and cut off the flow of creative libido. He leaves me as desiccated as a dead leaf in the fall, uninspired, convinced of my own banality. He kills joy, trips up my leaps of imagination so I fall on my face. He cuts the warp and woof of my weaving and wool gathering with a nasty knife.

And whose is the voice that speaks now, saying, *You're not being fair. I am the one who asks the penetrating questions that help you to think. And I might add, that's no easy task, what with all your intuitive leaping about, your falls into the depths, your serpentine meanders down below. It's my job to haul you out into the light and get you to see clearly!*

A Ghost of My Youth

I feel stuck. The easy flow in active imagination between me and my Sister from Below does not seem to be happening. How am I supposed to follow the flow of my images if I can't leap about, or meander? How am I supposed to play with ideas with a muse who will suddenly turn on me? Again it is a dream that intervenes. This time the realm of the dead is opened and I am flooded with memories of my old friend and lover, John Gardner.

John died young, some 30 years ago, of Type 1 diabetes. He was a wonderful ecstatic poet, an original in how he played with words. He supported my early development as a poet. The dream is full of the color red in many shades: magenta, burgundy, maroon, wine. I am given a poem of John's strung in garnets, as a necklace to wear. A poem which I have written for him has, in the dream, been published, in a magazine called *"The Fall."* I am to do a memorial service for him and read my poem. I am dressed in red. The ghost of John who had red hair and freckles seems to glimmer red and purple in the air. Standing at the podium I leaf through *The Fall*. Unable to find my poem, I am getting anxious.

John is a ghost of my youth. He was with me after I left a conventional marriage and set out to discover the temple dancer in my soul. He died in the late spring, early summer of his life, and I am privileged to live on into the fall of my life. But maybe the magazine called *The Fall* in my dream means something else. Maybe John is calling me from the world beyond to remember what parts of him fell into me, what parts of me fell into him. I've looked through the poems he wrote me and found two short ones in which falling is a central image. Here's one:

> I waken on fir boughs in the forest
>   underneath a bawning evergreen
>   sure enough there is a pixie lying by me
>   she rouses silent of the snow with the history of the forest
>   in her eyes
>
> she falls into me[156]

John liked to make up words, thus "bawning evergreen." He had a way of using common language to evoke uncommon experience. I love "sure enough there is a pixie lying by me." And by the time we understand that she has "the history of the forest in her eyes" there is a transformation. She who falls into him is a form of the goddess. Here's another John Gardner poem:

> I dreamed I flourished back in drenching turmoils from the land
> into the ocean of you and my spirit drifted into skies of you
> to fall upon your forests and do time as growing in you and begone return-
> ing to you I awoke for it was raining floriously out and
> freshning in upon me[157]

I hear that poem as John speaking from beyond the grave, returning to me, falling upon my forests, my tangle of thoughts as I try to find the path through these dreams and meanderings. And indeed, as I write this there is a righteous storm brewing, there are gray clouds, a wind that whips the trees around, and soon, the rain. I can see him. He was a slight person, more elf than man, not quite solid on his feet—his circulation had already been ravaged by his diabetes.

There's that male voice again: *Why are you invoking John? He was hardly a man. You were more man than he ever was.*

And then another, very familiar male voice, *Wait a minute!* John appears in my mind's eye, slight, with red hair and freckles. I can see that he is not in the least intimidated by that nasty voice. His intensely blue eyes gleam and he makes eloquent hand gestures as he speaks. He says:

This voice is masquerading as your muse and he's not. He is certainly useful, as editor, as critic, once you have done the body of your writing and need to shape it. But that comes later. You've got the critic, the judge who makes ethical pronouncement, and your brilliant scholarly father, all mixed up with your muse. Don't confuse him with me, John, your old friend and true Muse.

---

156   John Gardner, unpublished poem.
157   John Gardner, unpublished poem.

You don't want to commit the sin of seeing all men as alike, as many men have done to women all these years. Surely you can discriminate between the voice that interferes with your creative flow, and the voice that encourages it. Tell him to go away for now. Call on him later when you are revising your work. Then you'll need his thinking and questioning. Right now you need me.

Remember me? I understood your journey to unearth the goddess, to find her in yourself and in the world, to invoke her in poems and know her as your muse before you did. I explained it all to you. It does Her no honor to forget the men who have loved and encouraged you, the male poets who influence you, the male gods who fill you with passion. Remember me? I was the first to support your creativity, your wildness. Remember me? When you say a thing like, "There is no creativity without playing with yourself" you are invoking me. That's the kind of thing I'd say.

I do remember you John, and would like to honor you. I'm just not sure where I'm going with this. When I'm in the company of the Sister from Below, or other feminine aspects of my muse, I feel magnetically drawn to my writing. Though she is Other, she is also me. She enlarges me and I can be more me. But the male muse, even you, feel like you come from a different part of my brain. You are more other than she. I had a dream recently of dancing with a dark woman whose beautiful clothing was made of all the maps of the world. We were entirely in synchrony. We danced cheek to cheek. We dipped and twirled. Neither one of us led or followed. It was delicious. Perhaps I don't know how to dance with my male muse.

John glimmers at me with that glamour he always had, from another world. He gleamed and glittered and in his eyes I could see my own cunning, magical self. He says:

But you do know how to dance with the masculine. You do it all the time. Remember the temple dancer, how you knew and loved her? She wears red, is consecrated to the goddess, loves the god she meets in mortal men. Remember how it was when you and I were together in the early 1970s? Men and women were badly estranged. There were separatist women who hung out with you at the collective child-care center. Those women said they couldn't relate to women who related to men. They didn't mind me much. I was androgynous and harmless. But men were the enemy, and I could understand why. The patriarchy had done away with the goddess and usurped women's native power for five thousand years. Now there was a collective shift in women and you were all supposed to see things the same way. You didn't. You had the courage of your own wild erotic imagination, you were possessed by the temple dancer. You had even done a bit of erotic dancing—very politically incorrect. But you knew that this archetype was essential. You remembered the time when priestesses had sex, you knew in your body that sex was prayer and sanctification.

When God is a Customer

I remember, John, how you used to say that the ecstatic love songs of the 60s and 70s, the Supremes, Aretha Franklin, were about divine love brought down into the flesh. You heard it as devotional music. You understood that the sexual could be sacred and the sacred sexual long before I began to articulate such wild thoughts.

Later, after you were gone, I discovered the literature of courtesan poetry in South India. You would have loved what these poets were up to in their padams, a name for their poetic form. Imagine, John, that God is a customer! A john, a trick! That's actually the name of a collection of these poems, *When God is a Customer*.[158] They are written by men, usually in the voice of the courtesan.

In the Indian tradition of temple dancers, the courtesan, though looked down upon by "good women" as fallen, is educated, autonomous, can own her own property and make her own money. She is dedicated to the goddess. And the man who comes to her is a visitation from a god.

Sometimes in these poems the love is consummated, full of lust and joy between a woman and her divine lover. Here is the 17th century padam poet Ksetrayya, writing in the voice of "A Woman to her Lover."

> Caught in the grip of the Love God
> angry with him, we find release drinking
> at each other's lips.
>
> You say, "My girl, your body is tender as a leaf,"
> and before you can loosen your tight embrace,
>
> *it's morning already!*

---

158   A.K. Ramanujan, Velcheru Narayana Rao, & David Shulman, (eds.), *When God is a Customer.*

Listening to my moans as you touch certain spots,
the pet parrot mimics me, and O how we laugh in bed!

You say, "Come close, my girl,"
and make love to me like a wild man, Muvva Gopala,
and as I get ready to move on top,

    it's morning already![159]

A glimmer from the red and magenta glamour of John. He says, *You see, you know all about this archetype. You just have to find your way out of your own time, into the times of those who understood the divinity of the erotic connection between male and female. You know about the temple dancer, she is part of your psyche.*

Spirit Ancestors

A male voice says, *So, you know all about the temple dancer and her erotic imagination. But what about everyday life? In some traditions a woman might go to the temple once a year, to meet a god in the form of a stranger, but what is it like for her to return to her husband and children at home?*

The voice has shape-shifted. This is no longer John. It is the voice of a critical thinker. He raises an interesting question, but it's not what I'm writing about. See what I mean? When I engage the masculine I am vulnerable to being sidetracked by good questions, as well as nasty remarks. My creative flow gets blocked, the fire of my imagination is doused by a bucket full of cold water. I feel stuck again. Where am I going with all this? Again, it is a dream that helps me out of the doldrums. This time a dream about my husband. Dan is walking with me on a wide red dirt road. We are going North, where in waking state, I understand, the gods live. He pulls me up an embankment to show me the glorious red buttes of the Badlands.

This dream is pointing out the obvious. Dan is a different kind of muse, a practical one, who arranges trips to just where I need to go, often before I know it. So I need to write about a journey. Just to make sure I get the point,

---

159 *When God is a Customer*, p. 127.

I have another dream of Dan. In this one he is draping a necklace of grasses and seeds around my neck, part of a goddess worshipping ritual. This reminds me of a dream Dan told me years ago. He is holding a birth-giving woman on his lap. He is covered with her blood.

By now you'd think I'd get the message. There is a kind of male who loves the goddess, knows how to worship her, joins her in all the worlds. He is not new. He has been around since before the written word, since the beginning of human culture and the aboriginal cave drawings. Dan is in touch with this Spirit Ancestor. So was my friend John. When I engage this ancient guide in active imagination, he reminds me that I know something of the erotic connection between the earth and the sun, which is the most primal love affair of all. He reminds me of my experience at the Womb of Nenkovo.

Again it was Dan who showed me my path before I knew it. We were going to Bulgaria, again, because our friend Tedy Petrova had organized a Jungian conference on the Expressive Arts. For Dan, planning a trip is as creative an endeavor as writing a poem is to me. He had come up with a complex plan: first the conference, then a post conference tour of some interesting sites with other attendees, then our own private tour of the most ancient sites he could find in the Rhodope Mountains, the place where we had looked for Dionysus and found Cheiron and the dancing white goddess in her maenad manifestation.

Jungian Summer Camp

Now on a bus with fellow travelers, after having just presented at an engaging conference on the expressive arts where we wandered on charming paths amidst well-tended lawns and gardens, flowers and trees, in various groupings and pairings of Israelis and Brits, Australians and Brazilians, in the grounds of the former king's summer palace by the Black Sea. Many of us have become friends. Many of us are on this bus trip together. It feels like Jungian summer camp. The witches from down under, Joy and Traci, from the Chiron center in Melbourne, tell us the medicinal and magical properties of herbs and flowers. The Israelis' conversations flow from Hebrew to English and back. The Brazilians frequently break out into song. Michael, a young Bulgarian, says: "God surprises me every day." He wears his hair long, pulled back in a scrunchy, and says he wants to be limitless. We've all brought a souvenir from our bedrooms at Chateau Euxinograd: a little packet, wrapped in white with a gold image of the castle. It could be a little sewing kit. Open it and recognize a paen to the erotic—a condom! In each room, by each bed, an elegantly wrapped condom!

We pass sheep, goats, a young woman herding turkeys. We pass squashes, corn, cabbage, tobacco, apricots, sunflowers, roses. People are stooping in the cabbage rows. We see many stooped people on the land, in the villages. They look old before their time. But their land is so fertile. Every house has its grape arbor, its fruit trees full of apricots and peaches, its flowers, lots of flowers. We see a falcon, an egret, a stork in a huge nest of straw on the steeple of a church. Helga, from Germany, tells me how sacred the storks are. The farmers love them because they eat mice. They bring good luck.

There are so many levels of intimacy on a bus trip. We share toilet paper and give each other advice about how to use the squat toilets. Alice from Switzerland buys some rakija, strong Bulgarian brandy, and offers it to everyone. The Europeans and Israelis all have mobile phones. We hear Shane from England calling home to make sure her sons get off on their first day of school. Later we hear that her son has called to tell her he has a new pair of Adidas. Erel often talks to his wife in Tel Aviv. We hear the call he receives about a terrorist attack not far from their home. Our mood darkens.

Shane and I find ourselves suddenly in the wilds of the birthing room. I am telling her about the birth of a grandson, how he seemed to get stuck, how afraid I was for him and for my daughter. I tell her how an angel, in the form of a young woman resident, whom none of us had ever met, whom none of us have ever seen since, appeared and gently, patiently, oiled and lubricated my daughter's vulva and the baby descended. Shane has a similar story of giving birth. "How did we get into this?" she wonders. When we get to the Thracian Tomb near Kazanluk we understand. The Dromos, a narrow corridor, is a birth canal. You have to lower your head to get under the rock of the opening, like the pubic bone, to be let into the domed tomb/womb which is painted in Pompeian red. This tomb is a replica. The real tomb is fragile and we can't enter. However we are headed for the Thracian Cult Center at Starosel, excavated in 2000.

The cult center is built on a hill. It faces North, with the entrance to the South. It is made of granite and volcanic rock, and it is believed these two kinds of stone set up a pattern of energy. At the entrance is a ritual platform to the East, and high steps, as for sitting, to the West. We are told it is the biggest temple on the peninsula. The steps entering it are high; the Thracians were tall people. Only men entered the temple. There is an antechamber, and then an inner chamber that is entirely dark, built on a sacred rock, believed to be the tomb of a great king. Only initiates were allowed into that inner chamber. A wind flaps the plastic material which covers the opening of the structure. We enter.

I sit in the dark for a long time, opening myself, to a deep rich energy moving in gold and brown meanders. Suddenly, surprisingly, a familiar figure appears—a shaman in beige robes who came to me in a dream many years ago. In the dream he showed me the older brother stones. Then, he said, he had even older stones to show me, these were the older sister stones. He showed me that when a stick was dipped in menstrual blood, and used to write with, it would burst into flame. I understood that he was a male initiator into my own process of writing from the deep feminine. Now, many years after my blood has stopped, he is back. I ask him why he has returned.

It is time for you to learn to sit in the dark, to listen to nothing, to everything, to what the ancients say. Time for a woman to sit in the sacred place that has been reserved for men, the space that is female: cave, womb, tomb, grain basket. You are a shadow on an ancient wall.

I haven't thought about this dream figure for years. I am moved to see him again. I bow to him. He bows to me, he who showed me the ancient stones.

Dionysus at Perperikon

The shaman of the stones is with me as Dan and I embark on our personal tour of the Rhodopes, the details of which Dan has worked out on the Internet. Boris is our tour guide. He is a big bear of a man with a broad face, dark hair and beard, dark eyes that don't let you in. Socially awkward, he bristles with information and has a professorial tendency toward pomposity. Pavel, our driver, is quiet, doesn't speak English. Boris is good about translating Pavel's occasional remarks, and so we learn he is a man of the heart who understands our journey.

Our mini-bus is a rolling seminar on Bulgarian history. Boris had wanted to study ancient Greece and Rome. That was not the fashion when he was in graduate school. The communists were interested in glorifying the Thracian roots of Bulgaria. Alexander Fol was the leader of this approach. Fol was also the head of Boris' department. Boris has a deep aversion to him, sees him as a patsy for the communists. Suddenly it feels that I've landed in a minefield of Bulgarian academic politics. I struggle to sort out my orientation. Clearly, Boris is quite conservative, and very rational. Dan and I are on a journey to deepen our feeling for the Dionysian and Orphic rituals practiced in the Rhodope Mountains, which were holy mountains for the ancients. I've read Fol, appreciated his work and quoted him about the Dionysian mysteries.[160]

Suddenly I see that I am in an outer manifestation of my inner problem with the masculine: seeking the mysteries in the company of a scholarly professorial type. I do what I do in that circumstance—hide out. I don't tell Boris that I just gave a talk at the conference about my experience a few years ago in the Rhodopes, full of mystery and strange irrational occurences. I don't tell him that the archeologist, Ivan Marazov, was also there to give a talk, and said I'd caught the spirit of the Rhodopes. I am afraid that Marazov may also be an enemy of Boris'. I know what can happen to mystery when it is exposed to the bright light of logic, or the venom of thwarted ambition.

I consider that this might be a difficult gig for Boris, as well. He has already discovered that we are American liberals, against the war in Iraq. Unlike all our Bulgarian friends, we learn that Boris is proud of the fact that his government supported the war. He actually likes our president Bush. Now we will have to walk on eggshells.

We are going to places tourists don't usually go, places Boris hasn't been. He has to rely on local guides to tell us about the ancient sites that interest us. But he certainly knows his history. We learn more about the Moesians, the Dacians, the Gethians, the Thracian Period, the Roman Period, the Byzantine Period, the First Bulgarian Empire, Byzantine Rule again, the Second Bulgarian Empire, Ottoman Rule, and the Third Bulgarian State than I can stomach. I speak for myself because Dan has a historical mind and can engage in intelligent conversation with Boris on many of these topics. Meanwhile my mind wanders, watching the beautiful scenery.

Fall has happened. Peaches are gone, and now trees are heavy laden with apples and pears. We take in range after range of mountains, white clouds creating a turbulence of dancing curlicues. We are driving through tobacco

---

160 Alexander Fol, *The Thracian Dionysius.*

growing country. An old woman carries a sheaf of sun dried tobacco leaves, strung together, the long strands balanced on her head. In the distance we see a tower, Perperikon, we're told. We turn up a rough dirt road. On our last journey to the Rhodopes we had been looking for Dionysus, and never made it to the peak that bore his name. This time, armed with our own tour guide we are headed to the temple of Dionysus at Perperikon. According to Herodotus there was a temple to Dionysus in Thrace, which was as powerful an oracle as Delphi. Boris likes to quote Herodotus. Among intellectual Bulgarians is a feeling of humiliation about how late written language came to Bulgaria. They had to depend on classical sources to know their own history. But Boris clearly prefers quoting Herodotus to quoting Fol. He tells us that there has been continuous human life here at Perperikon since the stone age.

Our local guide is Milan Kamarov, a member of the archeological team that uncovered this remarkable site three or four years earlier. An angular young man with heavy glasses and an intense face, I never see him smile. He wears a blue T-shirt with Charlie Brown, Linus, Lucy, Snoopy and Schroeder all decked out in hockey gear. He wears flip flops as he leads us up the steep path through volcanic rocks. We wear hiking boots.

Perperikon is huge, and complex. We learn that it is the largest megalithic ensemble on the Balkan peninsula. Stone carvings begun at the end of the Bronze age were expanded during the early Iron Age. There is an acropolis, a palace or temple, sarcophagi, a village, and a medieval church. There are carvings and vessels from the Bronze age onward. Dan is admiring the drainage system. He and I have an agreement that he will keep Boris busy translating so I can sit and meditate. I see the flow of gold and green again, behind closed eyelids, and feel the presence of the shaman of the stones. Boris translates what Milan is saying of the religious practices. I get up to join them. Boris grins at me: "Have you found Orpheus yet?" He's onto me.

Milan shows us where the pilgrims bathed. It was a mystery religion. Only initiates were allowed in. A small evergreen rises out of a rock. Below, the fertile valley and the softly undulating Rhodope Mountains, blue gray. Milan points to the Temple of Dionysus, to the round altar where, according to Herodotus, the oracle prophesied that Alexander would conquer the world. Cut into the rock and rising three meters above the floor in the center of a tremendous hall is an enormous round altar, nearly two meters in diameter. Next to the altar is a square platform for the ritual acts of the priests. The hall with the round altar was built, the archeologists believe, much earlier than other parts of the complex. It has no roof and opens to the sky.

Longingly I look at the high platform, hard to reach because of breaks in the rocks. Pavel seems to read my mind. He gives me his hand and helps me over to the altar.

This is the ancient, uncovered part of the temple, where the ritual of fire and wine was practiced. One of the archeologists leading the work on this site, Nikolay Ovcharov, writes in a pamphlet about Perperikon:

> The prophesies made depended on the height of the fire, which flared up into the sky. But before the lighting of the fire a vessel of wine was poured onto the altar. This is the wine-and-fire ritual characteristic of the cult of Dionysus.[161]

I can see the young Alexander, the flames leaping up into the air. I can hear the voice of the oracle, telling him how much he will conquer. He is a figure of the older brother stones. I can see my own shaman of the stones, the menstrual blood, the fire. Is the wine symbolic of the earlier mystery that was shown in my dream?

The shaman speaks: *This place is much older than the story of Alexander. Your guides don't understand. This is the holy mountain where the ancients came to worship the sun god. Where we humans know we are the beloved of the sun. Where we create monuments to express our love for the gods. You've seen it in India. You are seeing it here. You will see it when you go to the Womb of Nenkovo.*

Ovcharov comments, in his pamphlet on Perperikon, that the "pressing and the processing of grapes is connected with the cult of Dionysus and. . . is a symbolic representation of him being torn apart." I find this comment helpful in thinking about the creative process and the difficulties I encounter with various forms of the masculine. Things need to be crushed, broken apart, stepped on, fermented, before they can become wine. So it went with Boris, our difficult muse of the journey. He and Dan got into an argument. Boris had made a comment about Indians, that they were stingy and racist. We had traveled in India with our Indian daughter. Dan could not let this comment go. He said that wasn't our experience. We had found Indians the most generous of people. Boris had stories to prove his point. Dan said he had a hard time with stereotyping, that so much damage had been done to our own people because of it. Suddenly Boris softened. He lifted his wine glass (we

---

161 Nikolay Ovcharov, *Perperikon: Chronicle of the Holy City*, p. 8.

were at dinner on a Friday night) and toasted the Shabat. He said *L'Chaim* and spoke of Rosh Hashanah, which was approaching. Later he would regale us with stories of King Boris III, who had saved the Jews of Bulgaria from the Nazis, and take us to the monument in Sofia—a tribute of thanks to the king and the people of Bulgaria.

There is another Boris, beneath the edgy intellectual persona. Actually, it is Pavel, our driver, who helps unearth him. We have come to see a healing spring. Boris tells us about the "owner of the spring," the god or spirit, who is a snake. He tells us that people throw coins into the spring to ask for healing. The spring is particularly healing for eyes, skin and stomach ailments. One of the difficulties of our journey is the Bulgarian tour company policy of providing us with fixed meals—huge meals. Three courses for lunch, three courses, at least for dinner. Bulgarian food is good, but heavy by our standards. So I am happy to throw a coin in and ask for some digestive help.

Boris picks up an old coin and washes it. He wants to keep it. "No, no" Pavel, uncharacteristically, intervenes, "the coin belongs to the god." Pavel seems to know everything about this holy place, and it infects Boris. Suddenly he turns into a priest. He takes a twig with leaves, lets the water from the spring fall on it, and sprinkles holy water on all of our heads and our faces.

The Womb of the Rock

Beside its human history back to the stone age, the town of Kurdzhali has little to recommend. It is not a tourist destination and the only hotel is an ugly high rise that reeks of despair and the old communist lack of aesthetic sensibility. Our room has a new rug, which makes it almost bearable. But we walk out into dark hallways with faded rugs stained with god knows what, into a noisy three sided elevator whose fourth wall is composed of the metal doors of the floors we pass. It makes forbidding thumps and creaks. Each time we hold our breath and hope it will click into its right place. We are on our way down for another enormous meal. Tomorrow is the big day. We are going to see the Womb of Nenkovo.

At dinner we visit with Boris, Pavel, and Mimcho who will be our local guide. Boris doesn't know anything about the Womb of Nenkovo. So how is it that my Dan knows of this womb? He learned of Perperikon during his many months of e-mail communication with the Bulgarian tour company. In the wisdom of the internet is a link from Perperikon to the Womb of Nenkovo. It was clear to us both that we needed to go to this ancient site. The owner of the tour company had found Mimcho, one of the men who actually discovered the cave.

Mimcho is a familiar. We have no language in common but I feel an easy resonance with his joyous enthusiasm about our journey. My inner guide, the shaman of the stones, must recognize him as his own. He tells us he does mountain rescue work for a living, but his passion is caves, abysses and old German bunkers. He writes a newsletter for children called "Rhodopi Equilibrium," which is about ecology. He had heard about the cave for years, Mimcho tells us. This area is Muslim and Turkish. In the mid 1980s the Communists forced all Turkish people to change their names to Bulgarian sounding names. Some of the Turks refused. They preferred to return to Turkey, including many of the locals who knew about the cave. The local people called the cave "noise in the rock." Archeologists looked for the cave for many years. They had almost given up. Everyone they asked said, "Yes, there is such a cave. I heard of it from so and so, but he's gone to Turkey." Finally they met a shepherd who would serve as their guide.

The cave was shaped by human hands to receive a fecundating ray of the sun. Mimcho said he had no idea about this thing with the sun. But he happened to be in the cave, one day, around noon, having lunch. It was March 22nd, the Spring Equinox, and suddenly a strong ray of sun pierced through to the deepest part of the cave. He quotes Alexander Fol on the relationship between heaven and earth in the Thracian religion, and Boris dutifully translates. Dan and I laugh: "There's your old friend, Boris!"

We have been worried about the weather. Rain has been forecast. As we leave dinner Boris points to puddles on the ground. We awake to clearing skies, and watch the sun being born through a gray blue vulva-shaped cloud. We are glad.

We leave the blight of Kurdzhali, the bleary, ragged highrises, the cement balconies festooned with laundry and drive into the mountains. The air smells fresh and clean. We pass through villages, sweet little clusters of brick and stucco houses. We pass a reservoir; the river is dammed upstream. We climb so high the clouds are below us. Pavel stops the bus. Mimcho shows us niches high up in the limestone mountains that go back to the first millennium B.C. The ancients put urns in those niches, with the remains of their dead. We come, at last, to the trail that will lead us to the womb. Pavel stays with the little bus. Mimcho, Boris, Dan and I start up a steep narrow trail. A black stork flies below us, over the river. Mimcho points out a stone temple high on a mountain, beyond the river. He tells us it is a temple of Aesclapius, a place for healing, open to the sun. Mimcho has a slow, thoughtful walk. His feet know the earth beneath him. But he is always, easily, ahead of us.

We take a break and sit on a log. Mimcho pulls something out of his bag. With great pride he unwraps a small clay figurine, a tiny phallus with eyes. I hold it in my hand. He says it is 3000 years old. He found it near the cave. He thinks it may have been used as currency. It is an enchanting little figure, with the simplicity and elegant energy of a fetish. Suddenly, with a mixture of amusement and embarrassment Mimcho realizes he has wrapped the little phallus in the last section of the paper, in an erotic photo of a voluptuous woman with naked breasts. This sort of image is a consequence of the freedom of press that Bulgarians have enjoyed since the end of Communism.

The trail levels off, then gets steep and difficult again. We walk over pieces of loose shale. Mimcho and Boris (who is remarkably agile for his big size) lend us their hands from time to time. A light rain has begun to fall. Mimcho says: "According to Alexander Fol, a Thracian temple requires a water spring, a snake, and rain." He tells us that before he found the cave the first time, he saw a snake. We look up at a rock which has a clearly defined vulva-shaped opening in it. Springing up from the rock at the bottom is a tree. Mimcho clambers easily up the rock, and attaches a rope to the tree. Dan and I gasp. We didn't know it required ropes to get into this cave. We are not rock climbers.

Dan says: "You go first so I can get a photo of you climbing up." I grab the rope with one hand, steady myself against the rock with the other, and walk my feet up a 90-degree angle. Had I been in an ordinary mode of consciousness, none of this would have seemed possible. But something much larger than my small, not very athletic body, lifts me. Then just like that, with Mimcho's help, I am delivered head first into the body of the Great Mother. "Super" I hear him say, his only English word. And then from below I can hear Boris translate: "You are the first woman to get into this cave!"

I'm not sure I can convey the power of this experience. The cave's vaginal shape is so familiar, known from forever, magnetic. I feel held in the earth's femaleness, drawn deep into her dark womb, filled with a deep sobbing. The shaman of the stones speaks to me now:

It is my spirit hand on the small of your back, under the soles of your feet that has catapulted you into this oldest sister stone of all. Here where the symbolism of sacred space is so embodied. Temple, church, mosque, all carry the same symbolism, but abstracted. Here earth is transformed into the flesh of the mother. This is no little clay goddess you hold in your hand. This is you, as a small human, being held in the Great Mother body.

I slept here. I had my visions here. I come from a time when men knew they needed to be initiated into this female place, the body out of which we all come, to which we return. Now it is time for women to remember her, to be born again in the mother.

I imagine the hands of Stone Age people lovingly creating this vaginal tunnel. There was a cave here, but it took the erotic imagination of the ancient ones to shape it so that the mother of all the gods could receive the phallic ray of the sun. I hear the shaman of the stones again:

If the earth were not beloved of the sun, where would we humans be? If the moon were not beloved of the sun, would there be tides, would women bleed? If the fruit trees and plants were not beloved of the sun god, what would we eat? It is the first creative work of human hands to cultivate this love between us and the gods we depend on. It is the primal act of the erotic imagination to marry the sun and the earth.

I feel glad to have had some time alone in the cave, to feel its power, to hear the shaman speak. But now I begin to wonder about Dan. I hear his voice. His shoes keep slipping on the rocks, he says. He can't get a grip. He tries again and again. Mimcho tries to pull him. Boris tries to lift him. But he's stuck. "That's Ok," he says. "The important thing is that Naomi got up." And he sends the camera up for me.

Boris manages to clamber up and I must return to the world of outer conversation. But I am glad to have him here to translate what Mimcho says. He points out the good acoustics in the middle of the cave. I stand there and say "Ohm." I can feel the vibrations bounce off the wall and return to the bones of my skull. Mimcho says the shaman lived here and spoke to the people. This was the "noise of the rock." The first opening, he says, the labia majora, is a natural cave. The rest has been carved by human hands. It feels incredible to stand in this ancient place and look out through the clearly vaginal opening at the slit of bright light, and the tree that made our entry possible.

I ask Mimcho if he is happy in this place. Yes, he tells me. He is most relaxed and at home here. Even Boris is clearly moved by the power of the womb. On the way back down the path a black and yellow butterfly lands on me. There are moths of a lovely periwinkle blue. No snake, but there is a small turtle by the side of the path. Once back to the van, Pavel drives us a short way down the road to a spring. We wash our hands. I put the cold spring water on my throat, my wrists, my third eye. I feel renewed. Before departing, Mimcho gives us a signed copy of his book on the history of this area, written of course, in Bulgarian. He tells Dan that I am a brave woman, and to me Mimcho says that he hopes my being the first woman in the cave will grant courage for my further work.

Later, in Sofia, at dinner with Bulgarian friends whose politics we know and trust, we asked about Alexander Fol. They tell us that during communism Fol idealized the Thracian period. Some say he manipulated history to fit the communist agenda. Perhaps he had to do that to survive. But since then he has changed. He does serious work. He is recognized as an important and reliable source.

So John, I have made a journey back to the time before the sky father took over. Guided by you, the shaman of the stones, and my own Dan, I have met men in the outer world, like Pavel, Mimcho, even Boris, who have helped me experience a female sense of self, and the power of the erotic imagination to bring male and female, father sun and mother earth together.

And John, a glimmer and aglow in his many shades of red, says: *You really should end with a poem of your own erotic imagination. I suggest the one in which you consider your own erotic history with gratitude for where it has brought you.*

on the anniversary of her first marriage

had i never leapt across the yellow grasses
of that meadow near Point Reyes to the sound
of the Hallelujah chorus never wound my adulterous
legs around my flute playing lover never been so blatant
so lewd i might still be married to that boy
from high school still be small and hidden in the pocket
of his green cordoroy jacket peering out at other people's
lives had i never danced to the bongos and the setting
sun at Big Sur never almost run away with that ferryman
masseur who could transport me to the land
of naked bodies and temple whore lore had i never been
such a bitch such a floozy never danced topless
in a bar never known the lotus flower
to blossom in my own goddess body never lived alone
with three children fed them eternal
soup of the week never been apprenticed
to a witch studied spells and incantations never sat on a wooden
floor howling with what came to me out of a cave never seen yellow
bellied death sitting on my bed forcing me to face
my real life—get up wash face bring fever down stay alive
to raise the children—would i have found my place in this sweet
bed where wanton and wild are loved by a man
who has light in his eyes where tigers and lions roam yellow hills
in my dreams and both sun and moon shine upon me[162]

---

162 Lowinsky, Published in *Rattle* and in *After Shocks: The Poetry of Recovery.*

Bibliography

Alter, R. and Kermode, F., Editors (1990) *The Literary Guide to the Bible.* Cambridge: Harvard University Press.

Arrien, A. (2000) *The Nine Muses.* New York: Jeremy P. Tarcher/Putnam.

Astrachan, G. (1992) "Orpheus, the Lyre Player." *Harvest.*

Bhartrihari and Bilhana (1993) *The Hermit and the Love-Thief.* Translated from the Sanskrit by Barbara Stoller Miller. New Delhi: Penguin Books India.

Bowra, C. M. (1961) *Greek Lyric Poetry.* Oxford University Press.

Broch, H. (1953) *Die Heimkehr des Vergil,* Neue Rundschau 64.

Campbell E. (1975) *The Anchor Bible Ruth.* New York: Doubleday.

Celan, P. (2001) *Selected Poems and Prose.* New York: W.W. Norton.

Celan, P. and Sachs, N. (1995) Correspondence. New York: Sheep Meadow Press.

Danièlou, A. (1991) *The Myths and Gods of India.* Rochester, Vermont: Inner Traditions.

Dante, *Inferno,* (1996) translated by John Ciardi. New York: Modern Library.

Dickinson, E. (1960) *The Complete Poems.* Boston: Little Brown and Co.

Doolittle, H. (H.D.) (1969) *The Gift.* New York: New Directions.

———— (1982) *Notes on Thought and Vision & The Wise Sappho.* San Francisco: City Lights Books.

———— (1988) *Selected Poems.* New York: New Directions.

Doty, M. (2006) "The Singer Sung." Review of Rilke's Orpheus in *The Guardian,* Nov 11.

Duncan, R. (1955) *Fictive Certainties.* New York: New Directions.

———— (1984) *Ground Work: Before the War.* New York: New Directions.

Eliade, M. (1978) *Zalmoxis, the Vanishing God: Comparative Studies in the Religions and Folklore of Dacia and Eastern Europe.* Chicago: University of Chicago Press.

Eliot, T.S. (1971) *The* Complete *Poems and Plays.* New York: Harcourt, Brace and World, Inc.

Felstiner, J. (2001) *Paul Celan: Poet, Survivor, Jew.* New Haven: Yale University Press.

Fol, A. (1994) *The Thracian Dionysus. Book Two: Sabazios.* Sofia, Bulgaria: Sofia University Press.

Gadon, E. (1989) *The Once and Future Goddess.* Harper and Row.

Gass, W. (2000) *Reading Rilke.* New York: Basic Books.

Grahn, J. (1985) *The Highest Apple: Sappho and the Lesbian Poetic Tradition.* San Francisco: Spinsters Ink.

———— (1977) *She Who.* Oakland, CA: Diana Press. p.5

Graves, R. (1999) *The White Goddess.* New York: Farrar, Straus and Giroux.

Henderson, J. (1964) "Ancient Myths and Modern Man" in *Man and His Symbols.* New York: Doubleday.

———— (1967) *Thresholds of Initiation.* Middletown, Connecticut: Wesleyan University Press.

Henderson, J. and Oakes, M. (1990) *The Wisdom of the Serpent.* Princeton University Press.

Hillel, R. (1997) *The Redemption of the Feminine Erotic Soul.* Nicolas–Hayes.

Hirshfield, J. editor (1994) *Women in Praise of the Sacred.* New York: HarperCollins.

Homer (1990) *The Odyssey.* Translated by Robert Fitzgerald. New York: Vintage Classics.

Johnson, B. (1981*) Lady of the Beasts.* San Francisco: Harper & Row.

Jung, C.G. (1975) *Letters*, Vol. 2. Princeton University Press.

———— (1969) *Collected Works*, Vol. 9.i. Princeton: Bollingen.

———— (1976) *Collected Works*, Vol. 14. Princeton: Bollingen Second Edition.

———— (1965) *Memories, Dreams, Reflections.* New York: Vintage Books.

Kerenyi, C. (1955) *Mysteries of the Kabeiroi.* In J. Campbell (Ed.), *The Mysteries.* Princeton, NJ: Princeton University Press.

Levertov, D. (1995) 'Origins of a Poem,' in Hall, D. *Claims for Poetry.* Ann Arbor: University of Michigan Press.

Lewis, R.B.W. (1995) *The City of Florence.* New York: Henry Holt and Co.

Lowinsky, E. (1989) *Music in the Culture of the Renaissance.* University of Chicago Press.

Lowinsky, N. (2004) *a maze.* Modest Proposal.

———— (2005) *crimes of the dreamer.* Oakland, CA: Scarlet Tanager Books.

———— (2000) *red clay is talking.* Oakland, CA: Scarlet Tanager Books.

———— (1992) *Stories from the Motherline:* Los Angeles: Jermey Tarcher.

Marazov, I. (1996) *The Rogozen Treasure.* Sofia, Bulgaria: Sekor Company.

Meador, B. (1986) "The Thesmophoria: A Woman's Ritual" in *Psychological Perspectives*, Vol. 17 #1.802

———— (1992) *Uncursing the Dark.* Wilmette, Il: Chiron Publications.

Michaels, A. (1998) *Fugitive Pieces.* New York: Vintage International.

Neruda, P. (1990) *Selected Poems.* Boston: Houghton Mifflin.

Otto, W. (1965). *Dionysus: Myth and Cult.* Dallas, TX: Spring Publications.

Ovcharov, N. (2005) *Perperikon: Chronicle of the Holy City.* Sofia: National Museum of Bulgarian Books and Polygrafy.

Patai, R. (1990) *The Hebrew Goddess.* Wayne State University Press.

Perera, S. (1981) *Descent to the Goddess.* Toronto: Inner City Books.

Prabhavananda, S. (1979). *The Spiritual Heritage of India.* Hollywood: Vedanta Press.

Rilke, R. (1989) *Selected Poems.* Translated by Stephen Mitchell. New York: Vintage International.

Sachs, N. (1967) *O the Chimneys.* Philadelphia: The Jewish Publication Society of America.

Sappho Translated by Mary Barnard, (1958) Berkeley: University of California Press,

Sappho: A Garland.(1993) Translated by Jim Powell. New York: Farrar, Straus and Giroux

Shearer, A. (1993). *The Hindu Vision.* Thames and Hudson.

Shelleda, L. *In the Shadow of its Wings.* Unpublished manuscript.

Tagore, R. (1961) *A Tagore Reader.* New York: The MacMillan Company.

Tukaram. (1991) *Says Tuka: Selected Poetry of Tukaram.* Translated from the Marathi by Dilip Chitre. New Delhi: Penguin Books, India.

Warden, J. editor (1982). *Orpheus: The Metamorphosis of a Myth.* Toronto: University of Toronto.

Watts, A.(1971) *Erotic Spirituality: The Vision of Konarak.* New York: MacMillan.

Whitman, W. (2001) *Leaves of Grass.* New York: The Modern Library.

Wright, C. (2002) *A Short History of the Shadow.* New York: Farrar, Straus, and Giroux.

Zimmer, H. (1951) *The Philosophies of India.* Princeton University Press.

INDEX

Also by Naomi Ruth Lowinsky:

The Motherline:
Every Woman's Journey to find Her Female Roots

ISBN 978-0-9810344-6-1

"(In) this perceptive and penetrating study . . . (Naomi Ruth Lowinsky) imaginatively applies Jungian, feminist and literary approaches to popular attitudes about . . . mothers and daughters and movingly, to personal experience."

—*Publisher's Weekly*

"A combination of years of scholarship and recordings of personal journeys, this book belongs in every woman's psychology/spirituality collection."

—*Library Journal*

"In this accessible volume, Jungian psychologist Lowinsky explores the pain that women feel when their mother-love is undervalued or erased."

—*ALA Booklist*

Fisher King Press is pleased to present the following
recently published Jungian titles for your consideration:

The Sister from Below	ISBN 978-0-9810344-2-3
by Naomi Ruth Lowinsky	Jungian Perspective
The Motherline	ISBN 978-0-9810344-6-1
by Naomi Ruth Lowinsky	Jungian Perspective
The Creative Soul	ISBN 978-0-9810344-4-7
by Lawrence H. Staples	Jungian Perspective
Guilt with a Twist	ISBN 978-0-9776076-4-8
by Lawrence H. Staples	Jungian Perspective
Enemy, Cripple & Beggar	ISBN 978-0-9776076-7-9
by Erel Shalit	Jungian Perspective
Re-Imagining Mary	ISBN 978-0-9810344-1-6
by Mariann Burke	Jungian Perspective
Resurrecting the Unicorn	ISBN 978-0-9810344-0-9
by Bud Harris	Jungian Perspective
The Father Quest	ISBN 978-0-9810344-9-2
by Bud Harris	Jungian Perspective
Like Gold Through Fire	ISBN 978-0-9810344-5-4
by Massimilla and BudHarris	Jungian Perspective

Learn more about the many Jungian publications available for
purchase at **www.fisherkingpress.com**

Within the U.S. call
1-800-228-9316
International call
+1-831-238-7799
info@fisherkingpress.com

1) Invocation to the Muse

LaVergne, TN USA
25 February 2010
174223LV00004B/163/P